LIFE
DISCOVERY

D.M. O'Dell

Harrison House Publishers

Tulsa, Oklahoma

Table of Contents

On this rock I shall stand

DISCOVERING THE LAW OF LIFE

We are all on a journey. We're going somewhere, or at least we're trying to. Sometimes the journey is really great and sometimes it gets rough for no rhyme or reason. It's almost as if the cold hands of random fate are cradling us for no consistent reason. At some point, we feel forced to look at life like we look at next week's weather. Who really knows what's coming?

At some point though, we all find ourselves in a place where we must ask the real question. Is there any real order to this madness or is life some long string of chance, compromises and deals? Do we even have a say in the final outcome or is it already being decided by some introverted and cold-minded organization.

There must be some kind of divine order. Justice has to be more than some romanticized ideal of folklore. Doing right surely is right and doing wrong cannot be anything but poison; there must be some defining standard that is tried and true. There must be a governing law of life.

Humanity has always sought to define its own path. I suppose being created in the image of God has given us the advantage of dignity desired, the heart and soul of ambition, but it also brought in the danger of self-will and pride. The truth is that God created us and placed within us an innate moral and spiritual law. We know to lie is wrong from the earliest age of awareness but that does not mean we don't try to get away with it and also feel guilt when we don't.

God has defined right and wrong; what He will bless and what life naturally rejects. He has given us a law governing life that is right at our fingertips. It is the Bible and it teaches us how we were designed to live by our Creator. It is the only place we will ever find true and lasting peace.

Oh, happy day when we discover that these laws are already so close to us; already written within us. The more we learn about God's law, the more we come to understand that we are not trying to change who we are as much as discovering and understanding who we have always been; how God formed us in the very beginning.

We are created in the image of God and it is through the knowledge of God that we begin to discover the true laws of life that govern the eternal realities of everything above the earth, in the earth and under the earth.

> His divine power has given us everything we need for life and godliness THROUGH OUR KNOWLEDGE of him who called us by his own glory and goodness.
>
> 2 Peter 1:3 NIV (emphasis mine)

Knowledge of Him

What we learn in scripture about God is what we call "knowledge of Him." It is given to us by God through the Bible. It is through this knowledge that we learn about life on both sides of eternity. This knowledge defines life as God intended it. These principles are great divine laws written into the very fabric of life itself. They are "Truth," lasting truth. They reflect the truth about the individual, about the parameters of relationships and about the discovery of faith. They reveal the nature of ambition and even dictate outcome.

As we discover these laws of life that God has set in motion, we begin to recognize and act upon principles that are designed to make us healthy and productive and to make a distinction between what is truly strong and what is fundamentally weak. God's Word is the simplicity of wisdom calling out to us every day.

Let's look briefly for an example at one such law of life found in Scripture that brings direction to everyday affairs. It is the law of seedtime and harvest.

"As long as the earth endures, seedtime and harvest, cold and heat, summer and winter, day and night will never cease."

Genesis 8:22 NIV

Reaping what we sow is a principle that will never pass. It sheds light on the way God designed us to treat each other.

Judge not, that ye be not judged. For with what judgment ye judge, ye shall be judged: and with what measure ye mete, it shall be measured to you again.

Matthew 7:1-2 KJV

Reaping what we sow is such a broad life principle that touches almost every aspect of our daily pursuits. It reveals God's heart in the way we should handle our relationships, our wealth, our

9

talents, our time and even our thoughts. It is truth designed to make us fruitful and this is just one law. There are so many others waiting to be discovered and unlocked.

We could also reflect on the laws that govern the seasons. Imagine the changing of seasons as you realize how life keeps us changing and growing in each phase of life.

> *For everything there is a season, a time for every activity under heaven. A time to be born and a time to die. A time to plant and a time to harvest. A time to kill and a time to heal. A time to tear down and a time to build up. A time to cry and a time to laugh. A time to grieve and a time to dance. A time to scatter stones and a time to gather stones. A time to embrace and a time to turn away. A time to search and a time to quit searching. A time to keep and a time to throw away. A time to tear and a time to mend. A time to be quiet and a time to speak. A time to love and a time to hate. A time for war and a time for peace.*
>
> *Ecclesiastes 3:1-8 NLT*

How eagerly we should recognize and embrace the changing tides of life!

Wisdom Cries Out

These are undeniable principles that govern every aspect of our daily walk. God gives us light to deal with both the seen and the unseen. This is real education. This is wisdom crying out from the street wanting to be heard and honored.

Discovering the Law of Life

Wisdom shouts in the streets. She cries out in the public square. She calls to the crowds along the main street, to those gathered in front of the city gate: Come and listen to my counsel. I'll share my heart with you and make you wise.

Proverbs 1:20-21, 23 NLT

This gate where wisdom places her seat represents life experience. It is the doorway where life's daily affairs are played out. It is out in public where all streets converge. Wisdom is out in the street of our daily walk where voices debate and life's fruits are judged.

This gate where wisdom places her seat is set along the way we go both in and out of public viewing and is filled with God's witness calling out to the simple ones who will but listen. The fact is that we need this journey of realization to discover ourselves as we continue the wonderful process of learning the governing laws of life.

Discovering the laws of life in the street results in the wonderful union of hope and faith to those who will but listen and follow. It is the final court of judgment where ideas and actions make covenant. We were lost and God is ever working to bring us back. You could say that the law of nature, in its bare brutality, is designed to lead us to the laws that govern us and dictate the terms of our relationships with God and with each other.

How I wonder at this new sunrise

THE GREAT TEACHER

*G*od has always used experience as one of His greatest teachers. I am thinking of Adam in the garden with God. He was alone with God but he had no perception of his solitude. He was happy and content as he was but God, who is good Father, wanted him to discover more, to grow, to realize. There is ever a new dawn coming to us all. I can almost hear the voice of God calling to Adam. What a sound it must have been; to experience that reverberating voice of creative power, of limitless intention calling to an individual. God is ever calling us, asking of us. He has needs, but He also has intentions.

Remember that He asked Adam to name the animals. The call of God came to Adam. He asked something of him and Adam simply obeyed. He had no idea that God's call to serve Him had put him on an epochal road of discovery.

Adam faithfully, obediently, diligently served God's purpose by naming every animal as they passed by. He gave names to the fish, to the birds, and to the land animals with amazing wisdom and clarity but still he did not realize God's intention. He had no idea what was about to come, what was lying just beneath the surface of his own life. Finally at the end of his task, at the end of the day, it dawned on him that each animal of kind came by in pairs of sorts. There were two kinds of each one!

They were male and female. They were the same, yet they were different. What could this mean? At some point, Adam must have begun to realize the truth about procreation and even more about God's design for fellowship as he came face to face with the reality that there was not one beast suitable for him. He realized that though he was with God in one sense, he was alone and limited in another. God led Adam to the dream of a kingdom of God's kind and he began to see his part in it along with the wonderful need of a woman.

Only after Adam had become aware of this new reality did God begin to teach him that it was not good for a man to be alone. To survive, you needed someone else. How Adam must have been elated to learn of God's dream to share life with like kinds. I can only imagine the cascade of ideas that must have been erupting inside of Adam as he began to experience the first signs of shared love, of companionship. It was not loneliness that he discovered but rather the beauty of sharing life with like kind.

There must have been a wondrous anticipation that flowed through his body as the idea of a woman began to take shape in his mind. The idea must have begun with a seed and then how quickly did it catch righteous fire as a new horizon was discovered. He was now ready to discover a whole new world that was always there in front of him; even inside of him.

Eve was not his servant like some men try to treat women today. She was an equal sharer in life. She was necessary for Adam's existence, for his continuance, and within their union he discovered the heart of his own happiness as well as hers. Together they were to share the responsibility of LIFE and even the pleasure of companionship. We know that they eventually failed in their responsibility, but that does not change God's dream and intention one bit and in fact, God never gave up on His dream of loving fellowship.

The fall of humanity in the garden is a factual part of our history. We are part of a fallen race, but God is still leading us by the things that we experience back to a right perspective of life. Because of the sin of Adam and Eve, we have a natural inclination in us to do wrong (Romans 5:12) that now is part of our DNA, but by the same principle, we also have a deeper desire to do right that is fighting to be embraced.

I love God's law with all my heart. But there is another power within me that is at war with my mind. This power makes me a slave to the sin that is still within me.

Romans 7:22-23 NLT

These verses in Romans 7 speak of two conflicting powers trying to gain influence. God is working with us to help us rediscover life as He designed it (Philippians 2:13). Everything that Jesus did and now is doing is designed to bring us back to truth; to redeem us from the bondage of sin and ignorance. God is helping us through the Scripture, through the Holy Spirit and through experience to redefine the way we look and respond to life's realities.

It is in this light that we are fearfully working out our salvation (Philippians 2:12), as He who began this good work in us will surely continue to help us to both know and to do what is acceptable in His sight (Philippians 1:6). He truly is the author and finisher of our faith (Hebrews 12:2). He is the Alpha and the Omega; the beginning and the end (Revelation 1:8). He is the word of our

Life Discovery

healed existence.

As we make every effort to be led by these laws of life found in the Bible, we are striving to stay within the parameters that God has set up. Leaving the Word of God separates us from His counsel, from His design. Departing from His wisdom is as foolish as turning a light off before performing an important yet dangerous task.

There is a correct way to deal with ourselves - our dreams, desires, fears, ambitions and so on - just as there is a correct way to deal with others that reflects God's way. Choosing poorly in life or living outside God's principles will lead us to loneliness and frustration as the harsh laws of nature squeeze out all that is weak and all that is out of its element.

The Andes Mountains

I remember living in Cuenca, Ecuador, a city which sets at an altitude of about 9,000 feet above sea level in the Andes mountain range, which is an extension of the U.S. Rockies in South America. To drive out of this particular city you need to still rise to about 17,000 feet above sea level before you begin the downward spiral to the coast. As you drive this route you begin to notice, among other things, the broad variety of climatic changes from the thinning air of this harsh elevation to the many types of terrain you go through in the descent ranging from treacherous cliffs made solely of rock all the way down to the fertile soils of the jungle floor.

Some of the lush vegetation we saw on the coast which was more tropical, was never found up in the rocky terrain of the mountains. The jungle below seemed to restrain no growing thing, but what easily grew down in the jungle could not survive in the higher altitude as greater demands were made on it. It is easy to grow things at sea level in the well-watered tropical environment, but the higher the altitude, the more challenging were the vegetative possibilities.

If anything, the jungle teaches the need for restraint while the altitude reveals a need for greater educated order. It is a wonderful picture of the varieties we find in life and the realities that we face. When the climate is harsh, there is more of a call to survive, to simplify. When the soil is fertile and willing, anything can grow and too often, everything does. Restraint is more important in the fertile soil than in the dry climates. Every season, as every altitude asks us to consider different things and the accumulation of these experiences again leads us to discover a broader, more considerate view of life itself. What beautiful gardens can be cultivated in the rich soil of Ecuador.

World-Changing Discovery

The Bible speaks of the Jewish law as a schoolmaster designed to bring us to Christ and God's merciful salvation.

Wherefore the law was our schoolmaster to bring us unto Christ, that we might be justified by faith.

Galatians 3:24 KJV

These Biblical instructions or mandates, like the different demands of various altitudes, lead us to truths that our minds must labor to understand and accept. They represent truth that was always there but was just beyond our ability to reason until we set ourselves to learn. Just like love is ever present in the heart of a youth, but it is only realized as the birthing place of true family as maturity and experience begin to have their way.

Puberty unlocks a great transition in the heart that is soon to change everything. We were not designed to be alone; it's not good to be alone (Genesis 2:18). Life, through an innate need for family and meaningful fellowship, leads us to our connection, not only with God, but with each other, all birthed through the need to express love. This is truth that was ever present yet unrealized until maturity opened the door.

Love Is a Law of Nature

Love is a law of nature we are only too eager to unleash in the shallow waters of base intention but often too slow to understand. The laws of life are powerful and they are filled with so many principles that unleash great influence and power.

I think of the courage that has gripped me in times when my children or wife were in danger. Before marriage, I never knew what willingness was inside me to confront danger but marriage and parenthood brought me to discover something in myself that was always there. Here I discovered a world changing law as I embraced the need to protect my own.

It makes me think of the zeal that consumed Jesus as He cleansed the temple.

When it was almost time for the Jewish Passover, Jesus went up to Jerusalem. In the temple courts he found men selling cattle, sheep and doves, and others sitting at tables exchanging money. So he made a whip out of cords, and drove all from the temple area, both sheep and cattle; he scattered the coins of the money changers and overturned their tables. To those who sold doves he said, "Get these out of here! How dare you turn my Father's house into a market!"

His disciples remembered that it is written: "Zeal for your house will consume me."

John 2:13-17 NIV

The temple represented Christ's very body which was a symbol of the unity of all believers, or you could say his Kingdom. This was what He came and died for. The temple was God's dream and somehow the temple leaders had not only failed to see this, but worse they used the temple to make personal profit. Oh, I can only imagine how Jesus must have burned as He used a whip to throw out those responsible.

This is yet another piece of knowledge that leads us on to higher ideals about life and about ourselves. Truly, in the volumes of the Book of Life, it is written of each one us.

Then I said, "Behold, I come; In the scroll of the book it is written of me."

Psalm 40:7

There was written into me a fierce duty to protect and defend the weak. The awareness of or the knowledge of my responsibility to my family helped me to make peace with the strength that was always in me; placed in me with a divine purpose.

It was nature that taught me the true perimeters of strength and then led me to understand why God, my Father, would suffer so much to save me, to care for me and why I must, in turn, fight the good fight of faith in the midst of a crooked and perverse generation.

Transforming Power

There are many inner attributes just like strength we are ever discovering and developing, such as the need to nurture, to grow, to build, to expand. All of these human inclinations are the source of great energy and transforming power as we see them through the eyes of Jesus. Of course, left outside the knowledge of Jesus they can equally become powerful tools that destroy.

Let's look at honorable human traits that find expression outside of the knowledge of God. For example, to deny fatherhood while embracing only sex is a shallow distortion of nature. We call that perversion. By Vine's definition, perversion means to turn away, to distort or twist, corrupted, to transform into something opposite of character, to change entirely. This is to say that to reduce relationships to a purely sexual interaction is to pervert God's intention which was clearly to reproduce, to nurture and train, to add value to society or the Kingdom.

It's not hard to see what havoc enters into a community when family values are lost or ignored. What kind of father can abandon a son? It's like sweet water and bitter water flowing from the same spring. It should not, no, it cannot be! It is a cruel reality working all around us as families are divided and children are brought up without fathers and mothers and taught to ignore God's intentions for a husband and a wife. This perversion of nature - this sin - can only bring death and decay.

The fruit of this perversion is evident everywhere. Nature cannot bless this. In the Bible, we see where sexual immorality was prevalent and it always brought in misery, decay and destruction. There is a law of nature that draws us to love and to companionship, to sharing and living as one, but outside of God's law it becomes a perversion that gives way only to appetite and as an unruly weed it produces the poisoning flowers of loneliness, division, malformed children and further confusion. This damaging harvest springs from a true desire for intimacy and love but it goes shipwreck without the knowledge of God.

> *Put to death, therefore, whatever belongs to your earthly nature: sexual immorality, impurity, lust, evil desires and greed, which is idolatry. Because of these, the wrath of God is coming.*
>
> Colossians 3:5-6 NIV

Before I realized this innate courage within me to protect the weak, I reacted out of frustration and fear during conflict because I was unsure of the reason and perimeters of force. I was ignorant. I did not understand. I knew cruelty was a bitter herb in my mouth while valor was sweet, but I was confused with such a broad variety of voices seeking to define my outward expression.

It was the knowledge of God that helped me define what was already placed inside me that set me free and the key was a life experience with family that included God's voice. God led me through this simple law of life to discover and define the nature of my own courage as I also began to understand His. This law of nature was my schoolmaster, broadening my life.

I think of Adam walking alone with God without the foggiest idea that he was without an equal companion. It had never been uttered on this earth that a woman could even exist. There was a truth ever present in front of him as animals moved in and out that he had not yet realized until God led him to a life experience. It was a dawning of a new law of life in Adam's mind. It was a revelation he instinctively reacted to. He was alone, but that was not the way he should remain (Genesis 2:20).

God calls us the same way. We hear His voice and respond.

We don't understand the full measure of His purpose but we obey no matter what the responsibility entails. Our individual abilities must be realized and unlocked and it is God's business to help us along the way. This is the beginning of understanding as revelation after revelation begins to build upon inspirations and realizations, as line upon line and precept upon precept begin to form in us God's idea of life.

We choose to embrace it. The Devil tries to distort it. This begins the trust we exercise in God, in His Word, in His intentions, or we choose to recognize other voices. Hope is not lost, it is confused, redefined. Adam's obedience unlocked one of the most important discoveries in history; the discovery of our need for each other and the futility of solitude.

The law of life has always been leading us to love, to unity, to one kingdom.

Thy kingdom come, they will be done on earth as it is in heaven.

Matthew 6:10 KJV

It is the law of nature designed to not only provide for us naturally, but to even lead us to God's ultimate dream of life. There is one God, one mediator between God and man and there is only one kingdom that will remain. It is a kingdom built of one body, which is the Church, and it is not to be divided.

The truth around us is merely unrecognized, undiscovered, unrealized until God begins to lead us to it. It is through a natural process of everyday life that we are enlarged as we work together with the Lord. God helps us to discover not only Himself through daily life, but He also helps us understand ourselves and each other. He created us. He needs us. He wants us. We create life because we need it, we want it. We have so much inside of us that we continue to discover as we get closer to God with each passing day, with each passing decision.

God had seeded within Adam a truth that marked the beginning of life discovery. Just as God created man for fellowship and for growth, so Adam now discovered his need for fellowship and growth. He was being led to greater truth. Written within the family unit is a divine seed that leads us to the greater truth of the family of God which is the Church, our spiritual family. In obedience, we unlock the untold reservoirs of life's riches.

Life experiences, both good and bad, are always leading us if we will only be led. This is why all things, though they be not always good, will cause us to glorify God if we can but see and continue to cling to God as He helps us discover the law of life.

And we know that all things work together for good to them that love God, to them who are the called according to his purpose.

Romans 8:28 KJV

And so the dawn did come,
bringing with it the treasures of old

THE INVISIBLE THINGS
OF GOD

*W*hen God created the world, He wove into the fabric of nature an image of Himself; a kind of picture of His own heart. As in every other thing He did, there was a reason and it revolved around His love for and his relationship with mankind.

The one overriding passion of His heart was to be with humanity but to accomplish this, humanity had to know Him, to understand Him, to see Him.

There are many ways that God labored to reveal His heart to the world such as through His Word, through His Son, through His law and even through people, but for the many souls around the world who have not the benefit of these experiences, then He has even seeded another way of discovering His ways and that is through nature.

For the invisible things of him from the creation of the world are clearly seen, being understood by the things that are made, even his eternal power and Godhead;...

Romans 1:20 KJV

Life Discovery

People all around the world from every conceivable social class are searching for God; they are reaching for truth, for absolutes and ultimately, for peace. As our creator, God not only knows and understands humanity's search, but He is profoundly committed to helping us on our quest. He is the life that we seek and He has been careful to never leave Himself without witness. Imagine how through nature He is testifying; leading us to truth.

"...turn to the living God, who made heaven and earth, the sea, and everything in them. In the past he permitted all the nations to go their own ways, but he never left them without evidence of himself and his goodness. For instance, he sends you rain and good crops and gives you food and joyful hearts."

Acts 14:15-18 NLT

Looking into Nature

Think with me for a moment about all that we can learn by looking into nature. Through nature, God paints a picture of life and death, power and eternity. There is design and destiny that is being laid out as a master plan for all to see. In nature we see the miraculous as life springs from life; we stand in awe of the power of the oceans and the imposing nature of their tides. We stand at the feet of volcanoes and tremble as the very heart of the earth roars. We feel helpless in the mighty storms that irreverently bring indifferent havoc and we can but look into the stars and wonder. In the course of a day, we might simply feel the peace of a gentle breeze or we might find refreshment in delicious fruit.

At times, we might even consider the harvest or the wonder of the seasons as the beauty of spring flourishes all around. We, on

30

occasion, might philosophically gaze at the withering body of the aged as winter changes the face of all around us with the steady, unstoppable drumbeat of purpose that is almost beyond our comprehension while the sounds of children innocently playing echo in the distance.

In the presence of such wonder and power we might become aware of the shadow of the all-powerful God who laid this all into being with but a whisper. Nature is passionately beautiful; it is brutal and it is final; it is as relentless as it is purposed and God has chosen to reveal a part of Himself to us through it.

Looking into the laws of nature can reveal to us universal truths about God's way of seeing and reacting to things. This even teaches us about ourselves and the way we interact with each other. These divine edicts have been left there like a celestial fingerprint designed to be discovered and understood.

In nature, we learn about social dynamics as well as discover the secrets of harmony. Make no mistake, God did this for a reason and His reason always carries eternal realities. What wonder is contained in the life that is all around us! God in His wisdom is helping us to both discover and to be who He created us to be as a people and as a kingdom.

Looking into nature is like reading the Bible. In the Bible, we see a picture of God and we begin to see a picture of ourselves. This image begins to unlock the mysteries of our desires and it even unlocks the motives and intentions of our own heart if we will allow ourselves to see.

For the word of God is alive and powerful. It is sharper than the sharpest two-edged sword, cutting between soul and spirit, between joint and marrow. It exposes our innermost thoughts and desires. Nothing in all creation is hidden from God. Everything is naked and exposed before his eyes, and he is the one to whom we are accountable.

Hebrews 4:12-13 NLT

Life Demands Justice

What is revealed by looking at the world around us can be as telling as good health or bad. When the world around us is not cared for, it can become unruly and sometimes even ugly. It becomes intrusive like a kudzu vine.

Life demands maturity and quality or it cries out for justice; appropriate interaction. Sometimes the things we see bear witness that we are on the right track, while other times we are confronted with the harshness of belated change.

Like a mirror, nature reveals the truth, not our shallow expectations. It's a miracle of insight right in front of our eyes. We can see people either happy or frustrated. We see children growing and learning about life in a positive, uplifting way or in a negative damaging way. We can see families either loving and sharing or tearing themselves apart with self-interest. We witness good politics that bring order or politicians that divide and control.

God has never left Himself without witness (Acts 14:17), and He never wanted us without awareness. He gave us eyes so that we could see.

Ears that hear and eyes that see — the LORD has made them both.

Proverbs 20:12 NIV

The Invisible Things of God

He has always sought to reveal Himself to the world and by this revelation, we are destined to discover what wonderful purpose He had in mind for our relationship with Him and with each other.

We see the forming energy of our own internal creativity that resides inside of our hearts and minds as the earth itself contains beneath its surface untold riches and resources that are simply waiting to be unlocked through knowledge and action.

The laws of nature unlock untold reservoirs of potential contained within a single seed as it is allowed to follow its designed course of life and death. Even our responsibility to give and to receive can be seen as we ponder the nature of trees and vegetation as they give both food and shelter, taking back from the earth without hesitation and without greed simply what is needed to live and to be.

Nature is but one of the many ways that God is communicating with us, helping us as a people to not only discover who He is, but also who we are as His creation; as spouses, as parents, as children, as friends, as members of our churches and even our society. It is incredible that through nature we can both learn about and develop our own godly character while we seed the same in the world around us.

We Need to Know Correctly

All around the world, people have labored to understand and define God. This reveals a basic human need to know the divine and to interact with spirituality. Here we find the root of the many religions around the world and consequently, the root of so much anger and division as people try to defend their own core values and convictions. This deep need of the soul grows into a religious fervor whether it is right or wrong and it fuels the divisive hate of religious pride and prejudice.

Once I was helping a man in Ecuador who tried to dominate his wife in every area of life. He was a good man who was following his convictions. He was not just a weak man who needed to bully. None the less, she rebelled, and rightly so, giving rise to an explosive division.

I talked with the man many times to help him better define his convictions but it was an uphill battle. It was terribly difficult for him to see beyond his traditions and his deeper seated convictions. He felt somehow that being equal with a woman was causing him to betray his faith. His misdefined convictions blinded him to reason. He was a good man who was poorly expressed.

For many suffering souls, the truth is what they believe, even if it is not true. Blinded by misplaced loyalties, it becomes difficult for them to change the way they think. We must reconsider our point of view in many areas or we will suffer the same consequence of ignorant convictions. Our love and happiness does not need to be sacrificed on the altar of ignorance and set on fire by the flames of tradition.

God sent Jesus to properly define, once and for all, who He is, what He wants from us and how we should interact with people.

Jesus saith unto him, I am the way, the truth, and the life: no man cometh unto the Father, but by me. If ye had known me, ye should have known my Father also: and from henceforth ye know him, and have seen him.

John 14:6-7 KJV

The Invisible Things of God

Learning about God is the key to progressing in life, in faith and in godliness. Discovering truth about God, the Creator of all life, is the same as discovering truth about ourselves. Seeing God anywhere is like looking into a mirror and seeing a miraculous picture of God's seed living in us and procreating through us. This happens through His Word and yes, even through nature.

It Is Natural for Us to Love

Discovering God is discovering ourselves. We are created in His image. We are the offspring of His mind and His character. We have sprung from the very seed of God. That is why is it so natural for us to love and to need love; to make commitments and to be profoundly disturbed by betrayal.

We are created from and for truth as seen in Jesus and any lifestyle, no matter how rationalized, that takes us away from this core reality is something that creates conflict and war and eventually death.

It is as natural for us to be like Christ and to produce life as it is for nature to produce all that is around us.

We are the offspring of God.

Acts 17:29 KJV

*...and in the reflections of time
our future was revealed*

SEED AFTER ITS OWN KIND

*G*od created the kind of life, "whose seed is in itself according to its kind."

> *Then God said, "Let the land sprout with vegetation—every sort of seed-bearing plant, and trees that grow seed-bearing fruit. These seeds will then produce the kinds of plants and trees from which they came." And that is what happened. The land produced vegetation—all sorts of seed-bearing plants, and trees with seed-bearing fruit. Their seeds produced plants and trees of the same kind. And God saw that it was good. And evening passed and morning came, marking the third day.*
>
> *Genesis 1:11-13 NLT*

The apple will always provide a seed that will reproduce the apple. In like manner, the loving person will reproduce loving people just as the violent will create violence all around them.

God created humanity with His image stamped within them, giving all people a tremendous potential activated by choice. Humanity is creative, possessive and sovereign just like God. Humanity will always reproduce itself just like God did.

Life Discovery

Knowing What Will Come

Remember, though, that we are not like the apple seeds. The apple reproduces after its kind which is apple, but we reproduce after our kind. We also have God's sovereignty imprinted in us. We have a choice about what we will embrace and this choice governs what we will reproduce.

By accepting and believing in God, we are able to release the wonderful power contained within us for good and for light but outside of a right relationship with God, we are helplessly reproducing the darkness and confusion of the selfish and frustrated part of us that is wandering away from Truth.

A seed can only reproduce after its own kind. It's a law of nature. As surely as God has stamped in you an image of Himself, so you are reproducing yourself in your children, your friends and your world and as relentless as the tides, you can be aware that your world is tirelessly working to stamp its image on you.

Looking at a fruit will show what kind of seed produced it and what kind of fruit will come from its seed.

In nature we see reproduction after its own kind, so also it is in human life. A simple exercise in awareness will allow us to see both where we came from and where we are going based on the influences that have been in our lives, the choices we have made and the telling fruits that have grown around us.

This is more than gifted foresight for the Christian. It is a simple and natural law written into nature and as easily observed as a garden. Understanding this law of nature becomes a powerful tool that brings clarity to the fundamental issues of life.

Seed After Its Own Kind

Learning to Recognize

Learning to define and recognize "the fruit" of a person, whether it is responsibility or integrity or any of the many definable qualities of character, puts us in a position of awareness that can and should direct our interaction with the world around us.

This does not mean that we separate ourselves from anything worldly or uncomfortable. It just means that we have an effective tool that helps us to guard our hearts. We become aware of the seeds that we allow to be planted into our lives and we exercise our life power by deciding what kind of seeds we plant in the world around us. We do this because we know that the seeds planted will always continue to reproduce after their own kind. It is an exercise in human responsibility.

Jesus said that we can know a tree by its fruits.

By their fruit you will recognize them. Do people pick grapes from thorn bushes, or figs from thistles? Likewise every good tree bears good fruit, but a bad tree bears bad fruit. A good tree cannot bear bad fruit, and a bad tree cannot bear good fruit.

Matthew 7:16-18 NIV

It is easy to look on the surface of a person's life and see charisma or talent. Recognizing potential has always been inspiring. If only we were judged by our potential. However, the truth of a person can be seen only in the fruits of their life, not in their intentions. After all, everyone has potential.

It's the fruit, not the intention, that is the glaring reality of what we really are. Like judging a book by the cover or a sports team by the uniform is judging a person by a smile. Many a young person

41

has found out a bright red paint job doesn't make a car reliable, just as a great big smile and kind words doesn't make a person a good friend, partner or role model. We can see in nature that apple seeds always produce apples the same as humans always reproduce images of themselves according to the simple laws of DNA and of human character. We leave our fingerprints wherever we go just like God did.

Who We Really Are

Jesus came to reveal to us the true picture of who we are and what we are capable of reproducing if we follow Him. He is a picture of God's dream for humanity and He came to help us discover who we were created to be and what we are designed to do. As we allow Him to carry more influence in our lives, we begin to see this image of God's dream for each one of us emerge as Christ is formed in us.

Oh, my dear children! I feel as if I'm going through labor pains for you again, and they will continue until Christ is fully developed in your lives.

Galatians 4:19 NLT

People are, of course, more complex than trees in that we do have choice and we do have the ability to be many things all at once such as children and parents, spouses and friends, leaders and followers and all this at the same time.

Sometimes we are both good and bad ground as we embrace one truth and pass over another. It's as if bitter water and sweet water were flowing from the same fountain (James 3:11). This should not be but we are forced to realize that it is a part of today's reality and at the very least it should make us oh, so grateful for the grace and mercy of God.

Seed After Its Own Kind

There are numerous areas of knowledge and various kinds of relationships and each one is like a field being plowed up, seeded and cared for. In each area, there are spiritual interests and natural interests. We are spirit, soul and body (1 Thessalonians 5:23), and all three areas must always be cared for.

We can develop our spirits and neglect our bodies or we can focus on our physical health and totally neglect our spiritual needs. We can develop our natural mind and neglect our spiritual progress. Further, we have relational needs with friends, family, spouses, fellow laborers, God and even ourselves and all these daily dynamics need attention in all three areas all the time.

Some fields, like relations, get more attention than others. There is God's dream for each circumstance and then there is our reality and life is the journey between the two points. Our desire to increase our capacity in any of these areas is critical. First, we must believe that we can improve and that comes only after we realize we should improve.

While being a good husband, one can neglect being a good father. While being moral is necessary, being moral in a single area doesn't mean that one is healthy in all areas of morality. All this paints a picture of who we are and what we are seeding in our families, in our workplace, in our churches, in our world.

By the priorities we set, we seed what is important to us into the world around us. At the end of the day we all pick our friends, we pick our priorities, we pick our bedfellows. We choose what we will invest in and what needs to wait.

This might seem a bit overwhelming or in fact it should seem overwhelming, but let's face the fact that we are on a journey to become more like our Heavenly Father, who in fact is......God. We are a fallen race. We have fallen from great heights that God is returning us to. It's a tall order we are trying to fill but one that we can aspire to since we are in fact the very children of God and we do, after all, enjoy His favor, His kindness and patience, along with His promise of help (Psalm 5:12, Romans 2:4, Hebrews 4:16).

And I am certain that God, who began the good work within you, will continue his work until it is finally finished on the day when Christ Jesus returns.

Phillipians 1:6 NLT

A Master Builder

Paul, as a master builder of people, labored to the end that the image of Christ could be formed in those to whom he was ministering to (1 Corinthians 3:10). The people of Corinth were but one field he worked in and what was left behind was the testimony or the fruit of his labor.

Ye are our epistle written in our hearts, known and read of all men.

2 Corinthians 3:2 KJV

It's a fact that the Corinthian church was known to be spiritually aware, but they were also notorious for being naturally gluttonous. The presence of such inconsistencies in itself was not the "tell" of Paul's ministry but the way he chose to confront it was. As a master builder Paul labored to respond to the deficiencies he saw in this church, allowing for their continual development and growth by planting the seeds of truth. He did not reject them as unworthy.

Seed After Its Own Kind

"Being perfect even as our father in heaven is perfect," (Matthew 5:48) does not mean we must be without error, but rather that we should be responsible or willing to respond to a circumstance according to God's counsel. Eyes see for the purpose of direction and understanding, not for a simple cataloging of facts. Maturity connects knowing with the appropriate doing.

It seems that Paul's fruit was less than perfect and that imperfection was seen by all. But Paul realized that what God was looking for was progress, not the clinical lack of error. God was allowing for growth by His grace and mercy. The world around us was designed to grow.

Realization is not license to judge but rather provides information that guides appropriate reaction. God gave us eyes that see so that we could respond to the world around us, not so that we could criticize it. Complaints don't remove the problems we face. They will never bring the changes that seeds were designed to bring. As a master builder, Paul was seasoned with love, patience, dedication, education and mercy.

He that is slow to wrath is of great understanding: but he that is hasty of spirit exalteth folly.

Proverbs 14:29 KJV

Of his own will begat he us with the word of truth, that we should be a kind of firstfruits of his creatures. Wherefore, my beloved brethren, let every man be swift to hear, slow to speak, slow to wrath.

James 1:18-19 KJV

Life Discovery

The End of the Law

What we see in ourselves and in others is not the end of the law. Jesus Christ is the end and the fulfillment of the law.

Christ is the end of the law so that there may be righteousness for everyone who believes.

Romans 10:4 NIV

The seed we plant in response to what we see is the plan of God working through us; leading us back to God's dream. The law itself was not designed to judge us but to rather lead us to God's ideal of divine standards. We can know what is good and acceptable in the sight of God and knowing is the first step to growing.

What is seen can be changed by what is not seen. What a fantastic picture of grace, mercy and patience. What is not seen is the idea or the Word that becomes the seed (Luke 8:11) that will reproduce after its kind if it is embraced with faith (Romans 10:17).

This is what ultimately gives real opportunity that leads us to a life change; hearing the Word of God and responding to it. The purpose of God's seed is to reproduce after its own kind. It is intended to lift and to heal; to restore us back to proper relationship with God by His own design.

This same Good News that came to you is going out all over the world. It is bearing fruit everywhere by changing lives, just as it changed your lives from the day you first heard and understood the truth about God's wonderful grace.

Colossians 1:6 NLT

46

Seed After Its Own Kind

Seed Power

There is tremendous influential power in life, in seeds. Realizing that seeds reproduce after their own kind is a fantastic awareness of life changing power. What we embrace is invigorated with our own life influence. We all have the authority of influence for both good and bad in the world around us. We are influencing and we are being influenced.

> *The field is the world; the good seed are the children of the kingdom; but the tares are the children of the wicked one.*
> *Matthew 13:38 KJV*

The seed is not only the Word of God, but it is also represented by those who carry it. We are all carriers of seed power; of seed influence. We carry the seed power to do good and the seed power to do evil. It's not that we are compelled to "seed." The fact is that we have no choice but to seed and those seeds will be either good or bad.

If we are among the living, we have seed power at work in us. There is no neutral ground. We are seeding our world as naturally as we are breathing. What a sobering reality to grasp the power of the influence of our lives.

Our lives contain potential forces of influence whether we realize it or not. We are building the Church or tearing it down. We are leading people towards God's Kingdom or we are leading people away from it as a result of our own actions.

Too often we use religion for our own gain as we value only what and who brings us personal benefit and unwittingly we become part of the corrosive process of compromise as we continue to cry, "Lord, Lord" (Matthew 7:21).

The law of seedtime and harvest is always at work in the lives of people. God declared that seedtime and harvest would always be a part of our lives.

"While the earth remains, seedtime and harvest, Ccld and heat, winter and summer, and day and night shall not cease."

Genesis 8:22

The world around us is changing and we are changing with it by this law of nature that God himself ordained. We can seed whatever we want into our lives and by this, we choose what we will seed into the world around us. As we choose the influencing factors of our lives, we determine the future of all that will be around us.

Seed has a life of its own. It is living to fulfill its destiny. We are destined to be influenced, just as we are destined to be influential. It is a law. Conformity is a natural part of our DNA.

For whom he did foreknow, he also did predestinate to be conformed to the image of his Son.

Romans 8:29 KJV

This reveals the power of influence as a natural law. What a life changing lesson we glean as we simply look at nature. This is not a generational blessing or curse passed on outside the realm of choice, but rather the law of nature in people that was activated by choice. This is not a generational curse but a generational choice.

The person who sins is the one who will die. The child will not be punished for the parent's sins, and the parent will not be punished for the child's sins. Righteous people will be

Seed After Its Own Kind

rewarded for their own righteous behavior, and wicked people will be punished for their own wickedness.

Ezekiel 18:20 NLT

Each person can change their world when they change their mind. We can change the nature of influence by a simple choice. This is real power. This is real authority. We answer for our choice. Realizing this truth brings intentional change.

The fact that family tendencies and traits are passed on gives further testimony to the power of relational influence. The element that ultimately activates and empowers this law is the choice that each individual makes as they, in turn, face the knowledge or the seed of God. Accepting the Word of God and acting on it is a miracle of change and even rebirth.

When one is exposed to a contagious sickness, one is infected. But how much more are we affected by being exposed to the life of God. God's life is powerful in influence.

It is written within the very pages of everyday living, a law that causes us to become more like Him or to be more like those we choose to listen to. We will always reproduce after our own kind and we each have the sovereignty to choose "what kind" we are. What a powerful lesson that nature teaches us.

It is God's desire that we be shaped by the knowledge of Him and that we shape our world after this same image; to seed the very world under our feet with both our ideas and our actions just as He did. Reproduction is a law. We reproduce what we are because it was written into our nature by God himself. This is nature's way.

Is such a sword designed to
take life or to defend it?

HUMANITY'S CONFLICT

*T*he underlying conflict of humanity is that we have all been seeded by both God and by sin.

> *Then God said, "Let us make human beings in our image."*
>
> *Genesis 1:26 NLT*

On this first side we have the seeds of greatness, virtue and nobility written into our hearts. Because we are divine offspring, it is instinctive for us to know what is good and acceptable in the sight of God.

Paul talks about a set of principles or "a law" that is written into our very hearts, that guide us through life; a code of conduct before both God and man.

> *Even Gentiles, (or unbelievers) who do not have God's written law, show that they know his law when they instinctively obey it, even without having heard it. They demonstrate that God's law is written in their hearts, for their own conscience and thoughts either accuse them or tell them they are doing right.*
>
> *Romans 2:14-15 NLT*

Life Discovery

This natural intuition is a part of every person born into this world whether born in the country or the city, the jungle or the metropolis. We are capable of knowing what is right and at the same time, we are also aware of that which is wrong.

There is a constant breeze of goodness running through our hair along with the looming storms of rebellion that are ever gathering on the horizon. These tormenting winds of darkness seem to be ever blowing through our world as steadily as the gentle call to goodness. It's unfortunate that from birth we seem to be more attracted to and influenced by darkness.

As a child, I was much more interested in an action hero than a preacher. If the action hero happened to be a "good guy" that was alright as long as he killed someone in the end. What a conflict of ideas I had rolling around in my mind.

The Bible teaches that when Adam, who was the first man, sinned he unleashed this tendency to sin on everyone born into this world.

Wherefore, as by one man sin entered into the world, and death by sin; and so death passed upon all men, for that all have sinned...

Romans 5:12 KJV

...for the imagination of man's heart is evil from his youth...
Genesis 8:21 KJV

I have discovered this principle of life—that when I want to do what is right, I inevitably do what is wrong. I love God's law with all my heart. But there is another power within me that is at war with my mind. This power makes me a slave to the sin that is still within me. Oh, what a miserable person I am! Who will free me from this life that is dominated by sin and death?

Romans 7:21-24 NLT

This is the epical battle of good and evil that rages inside of people everywhere. There is an intuitive knowledge of both good and evil within us battling for the supremacy. Torn between the desire for good and the inclinations for evil, we battle in our minds to choose the road we will follow. Whatever road we choose will eventually become mature or practiced knowledge that is born on the wings of experience in the direction we want to go.

The Journey of Progress

I am not saying here that we are all doomed to the fate of sinful man, because to accept Jesus is to accept God's salvation from this very reality. Jesus bore the consequence of sin for all of mankind so that everyone who simply calls on the name of Jesus will be saved (Romans 10:13).

...the same Lord is Lord of all and richly blesses all who call on him, for, "Everyone who calls on the name of the Lord will be saved."

Romans 10:12-13 NIV

Every person who has called on Jesus for salvation is free from the consequence of sin, but there is still a part of us that is learning to live without the practice of sin; continually becoming more like Jesus on a daily basis. This is the journey of which I speak.

Making daily decisions to draw closer to God's way is our great responsibility. The more in tune we become with God, the healthier we are in life, the better we treat people, the more peaceful our relationship with God and the happier we are with ourselves.

Yes, we do have within us the power of both good and evil, life and death. It resides in the inner chamber of our hearts where our ambitions and intentions are given life. Eventually this inner witness finds its way to the mouth and then into the daily journey of living.

> *The tongue can bring death or life; those who love to talk will reap the consequences.*
>
> Proverbs 18:21 NLT

God's Wisdom and Our Own

From the very dawn of human decision, we have struggled between God's wisdom and our own. As Adam and Eve sought their own path they released sin within themselves and consequentially, they released sin into all of their offspring. What an incredible testament to the power of seed.

Their intention was not to separate themselves from God but by rejecting His word, separation was the inevitable result. God will not let us redefine life in a way different from His design. The greatest eternal truth we can know is that we cannot reject God and continue with Him. Our wisdom is only truly wise when it is in agreement with God's.

It wasn't that Adam and Eve were unhappy with God and sought freedom from His control, but rather they were intoxicated by their own desire for what they thought was "more" or "better." Their judgment was impaired.

Most people are not unhappy with God when they choose

erroneous ways but it is their confused desires or their lust that draws them away. They think they can find some new sense of fulfillment or satisfaction in something that lies just beyond the boundaries of morality. Lust is when desires move outside of God's direction.

Temptation comes from our own desires, which entice us and drag us away. These desires give birth to sinful actions. And when sin is allowed to grow, it gives birth to death.

James 1:14-15 NLT

Emotional Influence

Emotions are a wonderful enhancement to life. They allow us to feel joy and even warn us through fear. Through emotions, we can process tragedy and even recognize love. The emotion of anger triggers part of our heightened awareness and we can even use depression to recognize the need for change. Emotions are a tremendous force in our life process.

Recognizing how closely intertwined emotions are with daily awareness makes it even more important to keep them under the direction of biblical knowledge. Unrestrained reactions are dangerous at best. We have all seen, if not experienced, the fruit of unrestrained fury.

Emotions unbridled will always emerge as the dominating force of the wandering mind. This unrestrained emotional process will become the overriding decisional force that, if left to continue unchecked, will produce the painful harvest of man's wisdom.

Convictions are formed when information, whether good or bad, is coupled with emotions and allowed to act. We energize what we believe with our passion and commitment. This becomes a willful expression of sovereignty; the path we choose to follow. It is the reality that defines and governs each person's sovereignty. We choose what we will follow.

Our choices are woven together with our emotions and then whatever decisions we elect to embrace become a life force; the dominating life force. That is why it is so important to let Jesus into our lives; to follow Him, to learn from Him, to obey Him.

Harnessing Desire

Lust is when a good desire goes bad; wanting things created by God outside of God's parameters. It is silly to think that somehow God is trying to make us miserable by keeping us from things that bring pleasure. Good gifts come from God (James 1:17).

Remember that it was God who created the flowers and the beautiful sunset. He is the one who made laughter and peace. It was in the Creator's heart to give us taste buds as well as sensational feelings. To feel rest after a productive time of work is truly pleasant, and let's not forget the tenderness of pure love. God made us not only capable of enjoying good things, but He made good things enjoyable.

Desire is the gateway to pleasure, but of course these things must be tools we use within the bounds of morality. We must exercise choice and discretion. We cannot unbridle emotions such as anger or love. They are designed to enhance our lives, not to control our lives.

Jesus gave us an example of how to bring human needs into agreement with God even in the most difficult circumstances. He expressed His desires but He kept them subject to God's will, trusting that what God wanted was necessary.

"Father, if you are willing, please take this cup of suffering away from me. Yet I want your will to be done, not mine."

Luke 22:42 NLT

Sometimes the limitations of human reason cannot see the breadth of eternal consequence, but the Holy Spirit is ever present and ready to guide us as we navigate through the ever changing currents of our feelings. This is what gives us opportunity to exercise faith and obedience in God's Word even when we don't understand all that His Word means.

Jesus did not want to suffer as a man, but He submitted to it as He knew it was the will of God, or we could say He knew it was for a very good reason.

Lust is simply perverted truth. Lies would never exist if there was not a truth to manipulate. Flawed determination is not always willful rebellion against God. It could just be a poorly defined attitude like the one that makes a man try to dominate a woman because he is a man.

To Err Is Human

No one in their right mind would set themselves against God. It is a self-deception (James 1:22). When our desires, our appetites, are not kept in tension with God's will, then we stray from agreement with God and we err; we deceive ourselves.

For I have told you often before, and I say it again with tears in my eyes, that there are many whose conduct shows they

enemies of the cross of Christ. They are headed
ruction. Their god is their appetite, they brag about
eful things, and they think only about this life here on
th.

Philippians 3:18-19 NLT

Peter had received the most wonderful revelation of who Jesus really was; that He was the long awaited Christ, the Messiah; the Savior of the world. But when Jesus began to explain the things that He would suffer, Peter became deeply confused; conflicted in his heart. This was not willful rebellion but it was an emotional train wreck of confused appetites that knocked him off the right track. His love for Jesus was carried away by his limited understanding of why Jesus must suffer.

There was a war in the mind of Peter between who Jesus was and what He must do, much like the war we face. We discover who we are as the children of God and then we realize what we must do because we are part of God's family. This is the arena where self-preservation battles with sacrifice for our spiritual family. This is where our passions are brought into subjection to the knowledge of Christ.

It is where desire is defined and embraced. This is the field where life wages its war with death and it is within the outcome of this battle that our fate is embraced. We escape the corruption of this world only by breaking these bonds of lust or unbridled desires.

By his divine power, God has given us everything we need
for living a godly life. We have received all of this by coming
to know him, the one who called us to himself by means of

his marvelous glory and excellence. And because of his glory and excellence, he has given us great and precious promises. These are the promises that enable you to share his divine nature and escape the world's corruption caused by human desires.

2 Peter 1:3-4 NLT

Leagued with Satan

Peter did react wrongly to what was in front of him. The Bible says, Peter took Jesus aside and began to reprimand Him for saying such things. 'heaven forbid, Lord,' he said. 'This will never happen to you!' (Matthew 16:22 NLT). Peter was unable to process the nature of God's willingness to sacrifice Himself in order to save those He loved. Peter did not understand and he erred. Peter had trouble finding the agreement between the knowledge of God and the knowledge that the world had given him.

Jesus responded without hesitation, as the Holy Spirit still does today, as a correcting voice of conviction. He both confronted Peter's ignorance and taught him by saying, "Get away from me, Satan! You are a dangerous trap to me. You are thinking merely from a human point of view, not from God's" (Matthew 16:23 NLT).

This was a heavy handed rebuke delivered without hesitation that shows how serious it is to mingle man's selfish ways with God's selfless way. Peter had no intention of setting himself against God but his separation from God's will in that moment sparked a very serious reaction.

Peter had leagued himself with Satan. Imagine! If this attitude had gone unchecked it would have reproduced the very seed of disagreement with God; enmity with God (James 4:3-5). Peter would have reproduced this life attitude of self-preservation in the world around him. This would be a very dark stone to build the Church on indeed. Peter lost this battle but we are thrilled that in the end he did not lose the war. He became a very powerful disciple in the course of time.

Discover Your Motives

What Jesus planned to do ultimately was never in question, but the way that Peter interacted with it was. Notice that Peter was not rejected or cast out, but he was directed and brought in. How many decent people find themselves working against the very will of God by failing to consider the nature of their own personal motivations?

How can we walk with God except we be agreed; that is, going in the same direction for the same reasons (Amos 3:3)? How can we connect with Christianity if our motivations and direction are not in line with God's expectation?

Adam and Eve struggled between their own desires and God's and in the end, they leaned left instead of right and sin was unleashed on that fateful day into their lives and ours with them. The ravaging effect of this seed in their children caused such a tremendous conflict in their lives that Cain eventually killed Abel in a burst of unbridled jealousy and passion.

Both of these boys reacted instinctively towards God but there was a struggle inside each of them with the influence of both sinful parents and a holy God.

Cain, as the seed or offspring of Adam and Eve, was torn both from within and without by the war that is common to all humanity. It is the war between the flesh and the spirit (Galatians 5:17). This is not a war that can be fought with sword or gun but only with the very Word of God which is our sword and our spiritual power as we accept it and live it.

> *For though we walk in the flesh, we do not war after the flesh: (For THE WEAPONS of our warfare are not carnal, but MIGHTY through God to the pulling down of strong holds;) Casting down imaginations, and every high thing that exalteth itself against the knowledge of God, and bringing into captivity every thought to the obedience of Christ.*
>
> *2 Corinthians 10:3-5 KJV (emphasis mine)*

The knowledge of Christ is the Word of our salvation. The knowledge of God, or His Word, is what was ignored in the beginning and it is what we must embrace in the end. Failing to recognize God's desires that were clearly expressed was what began this tragedy in humanity and it is only a return to the knowledge of God that will repair this breach. The Gospel, or the good news about God's will, is the power of God to restore life to all those that embrace it (Romans 1:16).

> *And take the helmet of salvation, and the sword of the Spirit, which is the word of God.*
>
> *Ephesians 6:17 KJV*

Choosing Counsel

Do we exercise our own free will to do what God has shown us? Do we choose to follow the right way expressed through both Scripture and the life of Jesus or do we try to find another way like Adam and Eve attempted?

A man's own folly ruins his life, yet his heart rages against the LORD.

Proverbs 19:3 NIV

The Bible shows us the end of each road through numerous examples of decisions made and lived out that can be traced through many generations showing the dominating and even prophetic power of decision. One author said the Bible was a true philosophical history because it lays out both the events as well as the far reaching consequence of decisions.

There is obviously a choice to be made as we see the lives of Cain and Abel contrasted. These men were not helpless in their pursuit of life, but rather each one chose what they would direct their loyalties toward. Abel's choice was righteous, or appropriate action, and he pleased the Lord (Matthew 23:35), while Cain's choices seemed to set him against the very Creator of all things.

The most tragic moment in the life of Cain was set during a moment when God was reaching out to him; God was there speaking to him with a passionate fatherly kindness, affirming in him what he needed to do to get beyond his inner crisis. He said,

"If you do what is right, will you not be accepted? But if you do not do what is right, sin is crouching at your door; it desires to have you, BUT YOU MUST MASTER IT."

Genesis 4:7 NIV (emphasis mine)

Accepting God's word confirms His trust in you. He knows your strength and capabilities. Acknowledging Jesus as Lord is to follow God's truth and His counsel, but to follow the evil desires of the sinful nature is to choose the broad road that leads to destruction.

Humanity's Conflict

Teach me, O Lord, to follow your decrees; then I will keep them to the end. Give me understanding, and I will keep your law and obey it with all my heart. Direct me in the path of your commands, for there I find delight. Turn my heart toward your statutes and not toward selfish gain. Turn my eyes away from worthless things; preserve my life according to your word.

Psalm 119:33-37 NIV

If Satan could possess you and make you do evil, forcing you to do what is wrong, he would. His authority, in a sense, is like God's in our lives. We must hear his leading and follow it. We are sovereign in our right to choose. God gave us that right and He has given us the time to decide what we allow to master us. Our ability to reason is God's gift to us as we choose who we will serve. Repentance only has value to us on this side of eternity.

Determine Your Fate

As a painful reminder, Cain chose his own way even though God told him he could and should master sin. God wanted him to win. It was the regretful result of Cain's choice to ignore God that unleashed his intense frustration and anger that caused him to become one who restlessly wandered the earth like so many others (Genesis 4:12). Unwilling to comprehend consequence, he threw his life into the chaos of what sin always produces: shame, regret and eventually death.

We are living the reality that we have produced with our own choices and consequent actions. This sounds harsh and insensitive but no matter how bad things get we must eventually choose our own path.

Life Discovery

My comfort in my suffering is this: Your promise preserves my life.

Psalm 119:50 NIV

Truth does not ask us to ignore the darkness around us, but it is designed to light our path as we pass through it. This gives us hope in life, knowing that God is with us.

In Cain's struggle, he chose to seed his world not with the life of God but with the expression of his own frustrated inner conflict; with the fruit of his own decisions. The law of life was at work. Blinded by jealousy, Cain pushed himself away from the wisdom that was calling to him, crying out to him wanting to be heard (Proverbs 1:20, Genesis 4:7). What eventually came from his unbridled emotional conflict was that he ruined his own life while he also destroyed his brother who was not opposing him.

The Ground Determines the Harvest

Our lives are the product of those that, like either Cain or Abel, have seeded our hearts and minds with distinctive actions or fruits. Some of these influencing people were associated with God's will while others, having embraced Cain's folly, have been the sowers of confusion and misery. So many seeds have been wisely sown in and around us while others recklessly have been strewn into the soil of our hearts by those who, "knew not what they did."

Jesus taught that ultimately it was the ground that produced the harvest. Some ground is hard, being unwilling to exercise the wisdom that is given. Some ground is shallow or uncommitted to truth while other types of ground are simply intermingled with the thorns of worry and fear. Still, there is always that type of ground which is good and rich; soil that is filled with the blessings of wisdom that spring from God's life (Matthew 13:3-9).

The world is filled with both good and bad seed that is represented by not only ideas, but more importantly by the people, the institutions and even the social movements that carry these ideas to the hearts of men and women (Matthew 13:37-43).

These ideas, both good and bad, are like seeds that have been ordained by the law of life to search for the soil that will allow them to live by the virtue of the law of life that created them; ever working to find the ground necessary to live and to produce as if compelled by the laws of nature to bear fruit. There is no neutrality. The law of life, like the steady pounding of the ocean's waves, continues to form the shoreline of our lives like a relentless force of nature.

There is a neverending tide that is determined and even destined to reach us and work its natural law of formation; molding us into the form of its beginning. It will eventually eat away all that is not rooted into the rock by forcing us to choose what road we follow, what master we will serve.

These waves come in the form of friends and family; in the image of education and social acceptance; taking the shape of organizations and institutions. These forces are shaping our dreams, our hopes and expectations; they are working to define what we believe in, what is credible and what is incredible.

The Force of Culture

These forming factors were with us before we understood our destiny with God; while we were innocent and incapable of understanding consequence. Our childhood was vulnerable, unprotected. These influencing agents, both good and bad, were our parents, our churches, our schools, our jobs and a list of other social elements such as friends or even the economic climate of our surroundings.

Because these seed carriers were so familiar and close to us, it became almost impossible to question, to challenge and to effect change. They wore the cloaks of tradition etched into the stone of heritage. We are a product of our environment and that is why God sent to us a great light so we could rediscover the power of choice.

Understanding this reality gives us not only the first recognition of "our true selves" but also the "why" of what we have become and are becoming day by day. This invisible force of influence is pushing its will in on us always; while we sleep, while we dream. It is the image into which our world has labored and is laboring to mold us. A force of goodness and a force of darkness is ever present. This is humanity's conflict.

And now deep calls to deep

WE HAVE POWER

*U*nlike the shoreline, we all have a remarkable power beyond the mathematical laws of nature, to choose the forming forces we allow in our lives and the extent of their influence, but being aware of choice is not the same thing as exercising choice.

Our choices are the source of our true power and they are defined by the voices we listen to and the things that we both admire and fear. These choices become energized by our courage and our strength as we act upon our predefined intentions. Circumstances are not consequences, but they do lay out the stage where consequences are debuted.

It is within the way we choose to interact with our circumstances, according to our knowledge and decisions, that life's consequences are made known. Our power is not in the knowledge but in the God-given right to choose how we react.

Walking in the Light

When the Bible talks about "walking in the light" it's not just referring to an enlightened mind but to an enlightened lifestyle (John 1:9, 9:5, 12:35-36, 46, 1John 1:7). Eyes that see are not merely eyes that can recognize truth, but rather eyes that can comprehend what is seen and react appropriately to it.

The hearing ear, and the seeing eye, the Lord hath made even both of them.

Proverbs 20:12 KJV

If we allow our eyes to see, that is to accept God's light or Word, and act on it through decisions, then we will begin to experience the kind of life God intended for us, which is life abundant. Real seeing connects understanding to results. This is what Jesus showed by example. He obeyed the Father in all things; even when it meant laying down His life.

Revelation does not make us better people but it does give us opportunity to make better decisions; the kind that have eternal consequence in mind.

Jesus is the light of the world, which means He is the light of every person who comes into the world. The light becomes the defining force of everyone who receives Him (John 1:1,4,9,12).

Jesus claimed of Himself that, "the Father and I are one" (John 10:30). Receiving Jesus IS receiving God, which IS receiving God's word of salvation. You can't receive one without the other and rejecting one is rejecting the other. Walking in the light is accepting God and His Word, while walking in darkness is rejecting Him.

Thy word is a lamp unto my feet, and a light unto my path.

Psalm 119:105 KJV

To accept God but reject Jesus is the same as rejecting God. To accept Jesus but reject the word of salvation is impossible. The idea that God wants to save you must be accepted or it is useless, but to accept God's word of salvation is to accept God in your life and that is precisely what unlocks your true power. Jesus came to bring us power in life. When He is embraced, He then becomes strength to the believer.

> *God can strengthen you by the Good News and the message*
> *I tell about Jesus Christ. He can strengthen you by revealing*
> *the mystery that was kept in silence for a very long time.*
>
> *Romans 16:25 GW*

The knowledge of God is the key to life. The ideals of the Bible are the defining elements that make things work right. Here we are defining light, abundance, and power as something that springs from knowing and embracing the Word of God.

Abundant Life

Abundant life is power; a divine resource available to us as believers. Let us clarify now that life abundant does not mean a life that is ever filled with excess of things, ease and harmony. Life on this side of eternity can be easily recognized as imperfect. These imperfections make us constantly aware of and grateful for our ever present help in times of need (Psalm 46:1). It's through our relationship with Christ that we are content with great abundance or in scarcity of any kind.

> *I know what it is to be in need, and I know what it is to have*
> *plenty. I have learned the secret of being content in any and*
> *every situation, whether well fed or hungry, whether living*
> *in plenty or in want. I can do everything through him who*
> *gives me strength.*
>
> *Philippians 4:12-13 NIV*

Life Discovery

Abundant life releases resources to us through faith that are supernatural. Our power to walk on the waters of this world's storms is a divine trait within each of us that is unlocked by a deeper and greater understanding of life facts introduced into our searching minds by the Word of God.

God's will was always the defining and directing force of the decisions that Jesus made. His decisions were so profoundly connected to God's heart that He was described as, "The Word become flesh" (John 1:14). God's will was manifest in Jesus. God's will is manifest in his Word and receiving it or Him is the door to abundant life. It feels so good to know that God sent His Word so that we could have abundant resources in life. We have wonderful resources of options and peace that the world does not understand.

I am come that (you) might have life, and that (you) might have it more abundantly.

John 10:10 KJV

The "I" in John 10:10 who came to bring each of us life is Jesus, who is the Word of God or that is to say, the mind or ideas of God. His word is the key to abundant life.

Abundant life is more than a Christian cliché. It connects us with resources, heavenly favor, and peace. Imagine the opposite; a life of frustration and emptiness, ever searching for a peace that cannot be found outside of Jesus. We have power available.

The Object of Power

It's interesting that Jesus, who is God in the flesh, did not consider ruling another man as something that was kin to greatness in life. He viewed authority and power in such a different way. He even taught that authority and power over demons was not something we needed to rejoice over. He was not trying to overcome demons. He simply was better than they.

> *And the seventy returned again with joy, saying, Lord, even the devils are subject unto us through thy name. And he said unto them, I beheld Satan as lightning fall from heaven. Behold, I give unto you power to tread on serpents and scorpions, and over all the power of the enemy: and nothing shall by any means hurt you. Notwithstanding in this rejoice not, that the spirits are subject unto you; but rather rejoice, because your names are written in heaven.*
>
> *Luke 10:17-20 KJV*

Jesus had a command of knowledge that left those who heard Him in awe.

> *And it came to pass, when Jesus had ended these sayings, the people were astonished at his doctrine: For he taught them as one having authority, and not as the scribes.*
>
> *Matthew 7:28-29 KJV*

His authority was not a goal or an ambition but it was a bi-product; a result of knowing. His authority was a fact. He did not need to prove Himself or be vindicated on the spot. He exercised a kind of authority that never questioned obedience. Such a knowing was so mingled with trust that it was part of Him.

The object of power is freedom. Jesus was not here trying to lord over people, but He was here trying to serve them; to set them free.

> *Then you will know the truth, and the truth will set you free.*
>
> *John 8:32 NIV*

Life Discovery

Truth itself was not created, but it was revealed to us. Jesus, who is God, is not a man that He needed to lie nor is He the son of man that He needed to repent. He is God. He is. His authority and power flowed from the simple truth that HE KNEW.

He created the world. He created the laws of nature and He created the law of life. He knows all of creation because He made it. He knows the heart of true happiness because He designed it. He knows the nature of emotions because He put them inside of us. He knows the danger of rebellion and the consequence and that is why He calls to us from the streets, pleading for us to follow Him. We must make peace with Him, with His ideas, with His truth.

We can choose to rise above the decay of human nature by believing and acting on good knowledge. This leads us to abundant life. We have power to choose who we will serve. We have power to live. We have real authority to choose the voices we allow to influence us. We have power to forgive and to release bitterness. We have the authority to move on and to change when we feel it is the right thing to do. The object of our power is freedom.

Through choice power, we activate the miracle power of God's good seed.

Seed Power

Seeds are ideas that become choices and those choices grow into actions. They flow from knowledge and experience and they are undeniable in their influence.

We know that a law of nature has been established by God to give seed both force and vitality and that simple law of life gives our ideas and actions influence and power. Our ideas are the seeds of our actions and they become the force in our lives. Better ideas, better actions; better actions, better life.

We Have Power

It becomes easy to accept that God's ideas are more than just powerful among powerful things. They are all-powerful and they are the defining source of our eternal power. When our decisions are connected to God's ideas, then we find ourselves connected to seed power.

Power Begins with an Idea

Power begins with an idea...that we believe in and act on. This is what unlocks the miraculous power of God's life contained within us.

But as many as received him, to them gave he power to become the sons of God, even to them that believe on his name.

John 1:12 KJV

This power, receiving Him and His ideas, is what helps us to transcend the decay in this world that we have all experienced; rising above the tides of despair though darkness is all around.

It is a miracle of life that overcomes the curse of death. This is what a miracle is; to walk on the stormy waters, to heal the incurable or give hope to the despondent; to raise the dead and even conquer the fear of death and a failed eternity; real power in living.

The miracle of choosing Jesus can even redefine our own nature. We can be born again, we must be born again. It is miracles that raise us up above the laws of nature duly established by God. He gave us miracles to help us conquer the evil that has been seeded into the world, but they are miracles we must choose to activate by our faith and actions.

This is the supernatural. It is the door to divine intervention in our lives. It is the law of new life that God has written within the very pages of nature that allows us to see hope beyond the corruption of this world but again, the key lies within our cooperation with God.

What God Believes In

Because we trust and believe in God, we can trust and believe in ourselves. We are, after all, the product of God's imagination, God's dream. We are His idea; each one of us. We came from His power and we are created to be powerful. We are created to be fruitful. God believes in us and so must we.

> *Herein is my Father glorified, that ye bear much fruit; so shall ye be my disciples.*
>
> *John 15:8 KJV*

> *Ye have not chosen me, but I have chosen you, and ordained you, that ye should go and bring forth fruit, and that your fruit should remain: that whatsoever ye shall ask of the Father in my name, he may give it you.*
>
> *John 15:16 KJV*

We are designed to be successful in the things we set our mind to do whether it is to develop good health, good expression, or good spirituality. We can trust in our ability to see and to understand as well as to choose and to be right.

There will always be those around you who try to remind you of your shortcomings and weaknesses. As children, we called them bullies. They were ever trying to control everything and everybody around them. They are not bad people, but just people who have bad definitions of what life expects.

They are insecure people who are afraid of any strength they see anywhere so they try to break it. They grow up and become frustrating parts of society as they are ever seeding their ignorance and frustration in the world around them.

Even though bullies will always be a part of your world, you still have the responsibility to choose what and who will shape the shorelines of your life. If you continue to listen to these voices that bring you down, you will eventually lose confidence in your own ability to gather information and respond with maturity. Negative voices will affect your ability to respond to truth and in the end, they will render you irresponsive or irresponsible.

We do need counselors but we don't need self-proclaimed lords. Each individual will ultimately answer for their own decisions. No one can answer in your place.

We must believe in what God believes in and that begins with ourselves. He believes in us. We must love what God loves and we know that God loves each one of us. It is wonderful to realize that the sole focus of God's faith and love is people from every nation, from every background. We are the joy that was in His mind that caused Him to endure the suffering of the cross.

> *Looking unto Jesus the author and finisher of our faith; who for the joy that was set before him endured the cross, despising the shame, and is set down at the right hand of the throne of God.*
>
> *Hebrews 12:2 KJV*

We can trust that the God who began this good work in us will not weary in helping us to grow. He does not weary in well doing. He loves each one of His children and He works for our good because He wants to; it gives Him pleasure.

He wants to put His life in the good seed that will transform your life. It pleases Him when we realize the truth and then act on it. He wants us to be strong, as it gives Him no pleasure to see anyone perish in weakness (John 3:16, 10:28, 2 Peter 3:9). God wants us to be strong. God's good seed is powerful. His ideas are life changing and they are available to all.

By faith we believe that by His word He created the world (Hebrews 11:3), and it is by faith we believe that He is re-creating our world through His words. We have the fortitude we need to walk the path of true life because He put that miracle into the soil of our hearts and it is powerfully working its design. Living a life of growth and productivity is not something beyond our ability. It is natural and proper.

We can believe in ourselves as well as in others. We can love ourselves and others. In this light, it is easy to believe that we can all achieve those things we desire because God is with us. The Bible is what helps us to discover this truth and it is the Bible that leads us to a life of productivity.

Freedom to Exercise Faith

These are the nations the LORD left in the land to test those Israelites who had not experienced the wars of Canaan. He did this to teach warfare to generations of Israelites to who had no experience in battle.

Judges 3:1-2 NLT

Even the difficulties we face give us opportunity to both see and understand God's Word, which leads us to respond in agreement with God's will. This is exercising faith and obedience. When we recognize God's will and willingly embrace it in life decisions, it is walking by faith. This is not a sacrifice but it is an exercise in wisdom, in maturity, and in trust.

We Have Power

It's not the force of our will and determination but rather the agreement we have with Him that determines the level of our power. It's not just our rational process but more deeply it is our rational process agreeing with Him. We allow the seed of His Word to fall on the determined good ground of our hearts and then, the seed realizes its destiny to break through our darkness and restore a life of fruitfulness.

We Find What We Want

We do have power whether we realize it or not. We are producing both seeds and fruits from the outflow of our heart intentions. We will always find what we are truly looking for, and what we find will produce itself in our lives and through our lives.

He who seeks good finds goodwill, but evil comes to him who searches for it.

Proverbs 11:27 NIV

And so shall be my strength

THE POWER OF AGREEMENT

*A*greement is more than the simple sharing of a few ideas in common or the occasional meeting of the minds. It means moving with intention in the same direction for the same reason. It is birthed from a deliberate commitment born on the back of shared knowledge and expectations and then develops into calculated action.

> *Can two walk together, except they be agreed?*
> *Amos 3:3 KJV*

This is an ideological unity that blossoms into a long lasting covenant of influence. Agreement becomes powerful when it becomes deliberate and premeditatedly purposed. When direction and reason are brought together by conviction, agreement immerges with the force of dedicated action.

Imagine a person who is motivated only to self-advancement. This person is attracted to and bonds with a social segment or a movement that advocates like principles and goals. Like a magnet, this person and others are drawn to core system of values, whether right or wrong. People of like mind attract one another. They move towards and cling to those who share the ideals that feel familiar to them.

Once agreement is recognized, then a bond begins to form. Support and strength begins to solidify and substantiate shared principles. Endorsed familiarity becomes the mother of validation. The world they have chosen to serve and honor endorses and corroborates the principles they live by. They advance and expand in the world they chose.

The power of agreement is a powerful principle that, in itself, is neither good nor bad, but it takes on the nature of that which defines its intention. You could look at money the same way. In itself, there is neither innate goodness nor evil. Money is simply a tool at our disposal, like a knife or like science. A person animates it with his or her own life or defined intention. The love of money defines the intention and becomes the root of all kinds of evil, but the wise use of money is the source of incredible amounts of good. The intention directs the outcome.

The Company We Keep

"The company we keep" refers to those we feel comfortable around. We naturally form bonds that will strengthen our position and support our convictions because we instinctively want to advance in our purposes, whatever they might be.

We naturally need and crave companionship so the law of life pushes us to make bonds with whatever or whomever we feel comfortable and safe with. The old saying that this brings to mind is, "a man is known by the company he keeps." This means that people are drawn to what they are familiar and comfortable with.

When a Christian person dates a person who is not a believer, it paints a telling picture of compatibility. True agreement is no pretense, but it flows from the convictions of the heart. Our friends become a transparent look into our own hearts. If you find yourself more often than not in the company of those who act in a way that offends you then the real question should be why are you continually choosing this particular companionship? To always feel superior to those around you actually does reflect the same ideal of compatibility. The superior as well as the inferior are both looking for affirmation.

Jesus set such a beautiful example in relationships. He gave the same honest attention to the Pharisee, to the Roman, to the outcast, to the poor and to the rich. He shared truth with the Samaritan as well as the Jew, to the men as well as the women.

He accepted invitations from the religious leaders as well as the despised tax collectors. True meekness acts without superiority. He forgave all who would repent.

There is a distinction between those you are reaching out to help and those you go to for companionship. We have all kinds of relations in the course of the day, but there are certain people we feel very compatible with or comfortable around.

The Demise of Reason

On the side of compatibility, if there is in a marriage a fundamental disagreement in values or morals or of faith, there will eventually be a show down. Sooner or later, after the honeymoon has been lost in the layers of time, there will be a fight. Those ideological clashes will beat a steady drumbeat of war. Eventually the disagreement will have to be dealt with and regardless of the outcome, there will be an inevitable distance between the two people.

Questions like what place the church holds in the family, the way finances are handled, the manner in which the children are raised and what they are exposed to and even how critical circumstances are dealt with will arise. Where would be the boundaries of forgiveness when convictions vary? How would love be defined, how would it be expressed and to whom? What would be the standard of morality? Would it be a mix of Christian values with secular ideology? Would right and wrong be defined by the whims of modern consensus?

> *Do not be unequally yoked together with unbelievers. For what fellowship has righteousness with lawlessness? And what communion has light with darkness?*
>
> *2 Corinthians 6:14*

> *Doth a fountain send forth at the same place sweet water and bitter? Can the fig tree, my brethren, bear olive berries? either a vine, figs? so can no fountain both yield salt water and fresh.*
>
> *James 3:11-12 KJV*

During seasons of unequally yoked relationships, there is no power of agreement enlisted and enjoyed but there emerges only irritation, aimless searching, discontent feelings and unhappiness not to mention fighting. The only real fruit from these seasons to be sure is the gradual demise of reason, conviction and life. This continual downward spiral will not stop until Jesus becomes the source of reason and decision, or we could say until we find agreement with God.

The Defining Factor

We are naturally moving towards what our own intentions and purposes dictate. We can feign superficial agreement for a while, but eventually what is in the heart will be seen and read of all. Our own deep desires and wisdom are the underlying forces that are directing the affairs of our lives. This is yet another reason to value more fully what it means to accept Jesus Christ as the Lord of your life. When the voice of Jesus becomes the voice that is not merely heard but obeyed, then He becomes the defining factor for the intentions of the heart.

Jesus came and preached repentance (Mark 1:15), or you could say that He came and told people that they needed to learn to think differently about life and He gave them the guidelines to do so through His teachings. It was a time when God himself sat down in the midst of His creation and let His mind be known. He taught humanity to seek first the kingdom of God (Matthew 6:33). To "seek" is an intentional force of will and "first" is the top most important priority. As a disciple of Christ, the Bible becomes the defining factor of our expectations and reactions whether they be personal, social or spiritual.

Knowledge and Loyalty

The Bible tells us the story about how David and Jonathan became such close friends. They had a "kindred spirit" or an immediate bond of love.

After David had finished talking with Saul, he met Jonathan, the king's son. There was an immediate bond of love between them, for Jonathan loved David. From that day on Saul kept David with him and wouldn't let him return home. And Jonathan made a solemn pact with David, because he loved him as he loved himself. Jonathan sealed the pact by taking off his robe and giving it to David, together with his tunic, sword, bow, and belt.

1 Samuel 18:1-4 NLT

Life Discovery

David and Jonathan had very similar convictions about their friends and their enemies. This bond of agreement led them to conquer many enemies and to endure great trials in their relationship. They only separated in the end because their loyalties had different definitions.

There comes a time when loyalties will ask you to deny deeper convictions and then the loyalty becomes something that will try to redefine God's expectations. We face some of the most crucial crossroads in life when we are forced to choose between loyalties and godly convictions.

Jonathan stood by his father Saul even when he knew Saul was wrong and this eventually led him to a bloody death at his father's side (1 Chronicles 10:2-5). Saul died because he was unfaithful to the Lord (1 Chronicles 10:13). David stayed with Saul for as long as he could until that loyalty threatened to take him beyond his heart's conviction.

I am a companion of all who fear You, And of those who keep Your precepts.

Psalm 119:63

Traditions

We naturally search for circumstances and people that are likeminded with us. This social network of agreement both influences and strengthens what we believe, whether it is right or wrong. Most people surround themselves with others who agree with them and anything that comes into this fortified world of accord that might be different can easily be met with challenge and resistance because of "agreement." It is a powerful concord that breeds traditions.

The Power of Agreement

Imagine the difficulties faced when confronting the traditions of others, especially when there seems to be a group of followers and supporters who believe the same thing. Religions around the world as well as secular ideals form dominating networks of agreement. The larger the group the more deeply the convictions root and the harder they are to challenge.

Media and secular institutions are enlisted to work together with traditions to create a formidable stronghold complete with endorsements and justifications. Dogmas become the guiding lights instead of developed knowledge and polarization reaches beyond the need for truth.

Bringing change into these fortified environments is a daunting task, especially when these views are supported by opinions instead of facts. Actually, when opinions are supported by enough people they will evolve into a "fact" whether it is true or not.

I talked with a man once who felt the Inquisition of the Dark Ages had merit because after all, God could help people change areas in their lives through suffering if they failed to change by reason. I know it does sometimes take difficult experiences to help us understand the value of godly choices, but to connect that thought with the Inquisition is ridiculous. Somehow I cannot imagine Jesus burning people at the stake in the middle of the town square or tying them up to a rack and stretching their bodies until their joints dislodged in an effort to lead them to love.

I tried to lead this friend to material that would help him form an educated opinion about what the Church and God will endorse but he felt that the material which was written on the subject came from prejudicial interpreters and thus would not bring value to the topic. This meant that his narrow minded emotional opinion was driving his convictions, not his education. Wow! I am glad he's not my priest. Agreement should be built on knowledge, not the whims of a half-baked doctrine of discipline.

Discover the Facts

Agreement is powerful and it should be reverentially activated after having discovered the facts. Agreement should be forged based on what we believe, that is in itself based on facts, not on what we are "supposed" to believe based on blind loyalties.

Morality for most is nothing more than a social manipulation of awareness. People do what they must to advance and they don't do what would seem to limit advancement. This kind of morality is not a conviction of truth but an expression of self-preservation. Morality should spring from our heart based on the biblical knowledge of what is profitable and what is damaging to life. Morality is not subject to what the trends are but it is objectively learned from the timeless truths contained in the Bible.

> *And be not conformed to this world: but be ye transformed*
> *by the renewing of your mind, that ye may prove what is*
> *that good, and acceptable, and perfect, will of God.*
>
> *Romans 12:2 KJV*

This gives way to the most powerful decision that faces anyone who feels a genuine responsibility for anything or anybody. People all around the world must face what they believe about God, about Jesus, and about the Bible and then they must choose the level of agreement that they will allow. The most powerful agreement that could ever be reached is agreement with God.

God does allow people to choose. He gives us time and opportunity to decide, but remember that this divine forbearance is not

The Power of Agreement

designed to approve of sin but rather to lead us to change. Reason is God's gift to humanity on this side of eternity.

> *His kindness is intended to turn you from your sin.*
> Romans 2:4 NLT

Some Forgotten Time

We can have agreement with God. I can think of no agreement that is more powerful than the covenant we have with God born of choice, not of control.

Outside of the knowledge of God, individuals seek unity with the kind of world they are comfortable with. This unity supports, empowers and condones. There is an old saying that misery loves company but remember, so does any other chosen disposition. Birds of a feather will flock together and at the end of the day, we all pick our bedfellows.

The point is that before we have Christ in our lives, we are by nature lost in our minds and we wander restlessly searching for the dignity that was lost in some forgotten time. We are easy prey to envy, greed and strife. As we wander through the darkness of our mind, we seek self-preservation and we seek what we feel will bring us stability and distinction.

The world that formed us so often was the unredeemed world and without the internal light of God's Word, we bonded with and naturally followed the lead of our surroundings that called on our sense of loyalty rather than our sense of educated responsibility. The evil world that formed us will ever try to keep us.

Religion and Agreement

Religion defines man's pursuit of faith and ultimately God. This in itself is noble if not instinctive, but when not seen through the eyes of Jesus, it becomes a cruel force of inescapable innate need. Humanity is born with an eternal spirit that has a profound demand for justice ever moving through the shadows of the psyche. It has been seen in every place and in every generation. Humanity is haunted by the spiritual, by eternity, by guilt. The need for sacrifice is a part of every religion and blood will always be found somewhere, showing the depths of commitment to this pursuit.

There is always a kind of sacrifice and there is some reference to hope. People of every age and of every race have labored to develop their concept of the spiritual and the divine and most of them have found religion to be a major part of their existence even if it was to challenge it. This places religion in a remarkable place of influence.

There have always been those who would exploit this deep seated human need for both spiritual truth and the relief from the burden of sin to find gain for themselves. How many atrocities have been committed throughout the ages in the name of God and how many people have followed spiritual charlatans, blindly supporting that which is cruel and evil?

> *A man named Simon had been a sorcerer there for many years, amazing the people of Samaria and claiming to be someone great. Everyone, from the least to the greatest, often spoke of him as "the Great One—the Power of God." They listened closely to him because for a long time he had astounded them with his magic.*
>
> *Acts 8:9-11 NLT*

> *Then Peter and John laid their hands upon these believers, and they received the Holy Spirit. When Simon saw that*

the Spirit was given when the apostles laid their hands on people, he offered them money to buy this power. "Let me have this power, too," he exclaimed, "so that when I lay my hands on people, they will receive the Holy Spirit!" But Peter replied, "May your money be destroyed with you for thinking God's gift can be bought!

Acts 8:9, 17-20 NLT

Simon the sorcerer lived off of the innate need in people to draw closer to the supernatural. Their undefined hunger made them easy targets of his manipulation. Even Simon was drawn to this lifestyle because deep down, he also hungered for God.

The world that created Simon was the world that tried to keep him, even when he got close to real truth. He offered money for the gift he saw because he only understood paying for favor. Being this way meant that the only way he would then help others was through some kind of payment.

Religion must be defined through the life of Jesus or it will become an expression of uneducated passion and conviction and eventually become a cruel taskmaster.

Jesus saith unto him, I am the way, the truth, and the life: no man cometh unto the Father, but by me.

John 14:6 KJV

Understanding Influence

God has given us the freedom to choose what we will give our affections to and this freedom activates our power of agreement. This power will work for whatever end or goal we decide and it will have long standing affects.

Life Discovery

Beneath our pretenses there is a real world of influence flowing out of us that is in exact agreement with our own motivations and decisions. This is a law. Remember that the seed reproduces only what it is. You could paint up an apple seed to look like a grape seed but it would not change what is produced in the end.

When we were young and tender, the world around us shaped our developing minds and hearts. We can now see what the world has done in us. In the same way, by looking closely at ourselves we can also see what we will inevitably reproduce in our world; in our friends, families and churches.

The knowledge base that moves us is what we will produce. If we fail to align ourselves with good knowledge, we submit to, through continued agreement, whatever it was that formed us in the beginning. Familiarity with our reality becomes normalcy. Sitting then in silence, we swear consent.

Recognizing and judging the true forming factors in your life is a daunting task; one that often has wings clipped by loyalties, naivety, lethargy, fear and insecurity. Nonetheless, the world that created us continues its relentless need to keep us, as if it had a destiny of its own. Empowered by peers and social agreement that is considered normal, familiarity becomes hostile to the freeing power of God and understandably reacts with hostility to anything that would challenge its validity.

Alcoholics are trained to say, "My name is Simon and I'm an alcoholic. I have always been and I will always be an alcoholic." People are so readily accepting the labels thrown at them like "ex-con" or "homosexual." These terms give identity. Imagine telling someone who has repeatedly fallen to alcohol and that has been trained in the "fact" of their genetic predisposition that they are not indeed prisoners of alcohol and that they can be comfortably free!

The Power of Agreement

When the system of indoctrination is challenged, a host of educated representatives release an onslaught of attacks against the simple message of freedom declared by God. Let me state though that before the world ever trained us in addiction, we were created in the mind of God and born in His image with the seeds of life already placed within us. There is a greater and deeper claim to wholeness written within us than the temporal claim of a dark season. When the testimony of salvation is given and believed, then a wonderful agreement is reached with God and the power to BE is unleashed.

Power Refined

Folly is bound up in the heart of a child, but the rod of discipline will drive it far from him.

Proverbs 22:15 NIV

Just as folly is bound up within us that must be driven out, so is remarkable potential lying deep within our hearts that we must recognize, define and develop. Remember that before the world ever stamped a label on you, God had already stamped an impression inside of you of His very image and strength; a self-portrait of true relevance that is rediscovered when Jesus is embraced. These life changing ideas are again activated by choices that we are more than capable of making if we only believe. Choose to exercise the power of agreement with God rather than agreement with a weak and limited system of partial knowledge.

According as his divine power hath given unto us all things that pertain unto life and godliness, through the knowledge of him that hath called us to glory and virtue.

2 Peter 1:3 KJV

Life Discovery

Integrity and dignity are as normal as nobility inside each one of us. This is an image that is unlocked with the knowledge of God, not by the recognition and favor of man. It is the word of our salvation; the message of the Gospel we hear and believe. It is the reality of hope we cling to in the night as God's steady testimony whispers in the wind. We are not changing who we are as much as we are discovering who we are. We do not change the world around us, but we discover the riches of the world right under our feet.

We are all created in the image of God and before we were ever stained by this world, we were destined to be as we truly are, the children of God!" Just as the law of life brought us harm when we walked in sin, so now even more powerfully the same law can give us NEW LIFE!

For as by one man's disobedience many were made sinners, so by the obedience of one shall many be made righteous.
Romans 5:19 KJV

There is a law of life that was written deep within us before any of these more natural impregnations such as alcoholism or violence or homosexuality or religiosity sunk their roots in us. It is the Law of God's Life. It is natural for us to believe; to soar with eagle's wings.

Before this world and our social environment began to form us, God had already seeded in us His own image. Remember that the invisible things of God are revealed through nature. There is something written deep within us that longs for satisfying dignity, for sacrificial relevance, for true spirituality and for wonderful miracles associated with even the common parts of life. Jesus brought this powerful heavenly influence into even the common areas of our lives.

The Power of Agreement

Something Strangely Familiar

That is why when we see Jesus, we see something strangely familiar. We see in Him a distant dream almost lost; nearly forgotten. We see an image partly through a cloudy glass that now begins to take shape. It's like looking into a foggy mirror or recollecting a distant memory or an old friend. This isn't so strange at second glance. We are, after all, created in His image. We are His sons and daughters.

The recognition of a healthy humanity becomes logical. It is why we are so deeply disturbed to see evil at work in people whether it's selfishness or cruelty. Even sinners hate injustice. This is also why we feel the war raging within our own hearts when we are unfaithful to this truth of predestined and universal divinity. In Proverbs 13:2, it says that the unfaithful have a craving for violence.

> *From the fruit of his lips a man enjoys good things, but the unfaithful have a craving for violence.*
>
> *Proverbs 13:2 NIV*

Could it be that the realization of inner failure is what feeds the violence and frustration in so many?

The seed of life has its own image written into it and it is seeded deep within our hearts. It was designed to reproduce after its kind. It is a law! As God's offspring, we have His very nature running all through us that our willful agreement will unlock. It is His life that thrives in our very blood. It is natural for us to be spiritual, to be sacrificial, to be like God. It is natural for us love, to believe and to even give our lives effortlessly for people we don't even know.

Coming Home

We are Christ-like and knowing Him is like coming home after a long and perilous journey. We must turn to Him and accept Him in our lives as the one true Lord. This is our power and it is as natural as coming home. How we all long for a home where there is love, harmony and truth. A place we can be proud of and believe in. A refuge where we readily bring the weak, knowing the wonderful rest and renewal that awaits them.

Do you know a person who does not hope for better in this life? Even a thief tries to improve his skills. We cannot find a person void of love. Everyone forms some kind of attachment to a thing or a habit, if not to a pet. Maybe it's to an idea that some make their bond or give their allegiance but believe me, it is an offshoot of a natural tendency to love infallibly. In Him we have power to become the children of God; having agreement with God.

While memories slipped into the shadows, the war did end.

MAKING PEACE

Making peace is an intentional decision. It is an act of educated reason. Peace is not a euphoric state of being but a result of good choices in a difficult world. We make peace in our own lives like we make a cake; we recognize the proper ingredients and use them.

Remember, we are not trying to change who we are, but rather trying to rediscover who we are; to get a glimpse of and embrace what God designed and created us to be. There will always be some internal area of thinking that has been misguided by confused ambitions but at our core, deep within our heart, we are created just as God intended for us to be. We can make peace with ourselves if we want to.

Some of us are energetic and explosive while some are pensive and premeditated. This is no conflict unless we have been convinced that one way is better than another. Some people enjoy leading while others find fulfillment in supporting. There are some who simply enjoy music, having never felt the need to create it. Not everyone is athletic and there are those who just don't enjoy sushi. The fact is that we are all different and being different is alright.

What is it then that creates the conflict inside of us? What is it that makes us so dissatisfied with who we are that we are eaten up with jealousy and envy? What creates the barrier between us and peace? Is it when we try to live in two conflicting worlds? Is it when we try to be someone other than the person God created us to be?

The grass does seem to grow greener on the other side of the fence, but once we leap over to the other side, it again becomes our side of the fence. It seems there is always something more that we need; something that we feel that if we possessed would make the "difference."

There are so many things placed in front of us that are supposedly great ambitions or great improvements that simply distract us from seeing what we already have. There is a never ending array of voices all around us trying to sell something to us by convincing us that there are other roads to fulfillment and peace and they all say the same thing, "This is it!"

The Same Old Decisions

I have lived all over the world and found that new places always hold the same old decisions. I have lived in the beautiful, raw islands of New Guinea and I have lived in the endless city of Buenos Aires. I have lived in the rainless desserts of Chile and in the beautiful mountains of Ecuador. I have lived in the ancient lands of India as well as the classical lands of Transylvania. Whether I was alone or surrounded by culture, I was ever working to find peace and fulfillment as if it were something "out there."

Now I realize that peace is something you find inside of you. Peace is something you accept when you finally allow God to open your eyes so you can see who you really are. Outside, there are voices that say you should be strong, you should be rich, you should be clever, you should be cold, but these voices conflict with that inner witness that leads you to the same old decisions of life like whether or not to be kind, loving, gentle, sacrificial, wise, miraculous and so many other wonderful things.

Outer voices say you must get while inner voices say it's alright to give. Outer voices say you should turn your back while inner voices lead you to open your heart yet once again, because you know you're not as fragile as the world would have you think.

What a fracas we have inside of us. The Bible says, "You cannot serve both God and Money" (Matthew 6:24 NIV). You will either serve the ideas of worldly stability or you will reach out to God's idea of stability. What fellowship is there between light and darkness (2 Corinthians 6:14). Light is God's counsel, while darkness is the conflicting counsel of this world's wisdom.

Peace Begins with Awareness

The Bible is filled with so many examples of right attitudes and wrong ones; good choices and bad. It teaches about the broad path and a narrow path. Aren't there sheep and goats, night and day? Weren't there stories that portrayed good servants as well as those who were evil? Some were faithful and true while others betrayed counsel and good judgment.

Some were humbly forgiven while others blundered along in self-righteousness. There stood those who were salty and there were some who lost their savor. This list is nearly inexhaustible because where there is a thing that is right, there will naturally be a thing that is wrong and this, in itself, creates the need for constant awareness and perpetual decision.

There were true prophets and false. There were lords and

servants. There were those who feared God and those who feared man. The point is that God sent Jesus to bring us to real awareness; a point of steady light.

Peace sits like a gentle flower right in the middle of this field of choices, right out in the open. It seems fragile but somehow it proudly stands tall through the brutal winds of mankind's turbulent searching for life.

God sent the Holy Spirit to be a steady companion in counsel; one who would never fail us nor abandon us. Our inner voice leads us to discover who we really are and then we don't have to worry about what others want us to be.

Making peace begins with being aware of God's way for you and then choosing it. He does know you. He did create you. Father knows best.

> *"I knew you before I formed you in your mother's womb. Before you were born I set you apart and appointed you as my prophet to the nations."*
>
> *Jeremiah 1:5 NLT*

Trying to live outside of God's way is a frustrating existence that gives no rest. The only place we will ever find peace is the place where our heart does not condemn us but rather tells us we are alright (1 John 3:20-21). We cannot afford to live to please man when that need draws us away from the voice of God. We must live to please God.

Peace and War

Doing the right thing can create trouble in the world around us but it will also bring peace. For example, disciplining my children does not give me pleasure but there is a deeper satisfaction knowing that I am saving them from the much trouble that comes from selfishness and unbridled emotions. They do not need to understand discipline as much as they need to experience it; to feel the reality of definition's counsel. Understanding will come in time when maturity and reason come of age.

I remember once when one of my sons had done something very wrong while we were out. I told him clearly what would happen when we got home if he persisted. It was a calm communication. He misunderstood the calmness for insincerity.

So when we returned home, I asked him to go to his room where I was going to make good on my word. When he realized that consequence was coming just as I had warned him earlier, he was stunned. He couldn't believe that after several hours, the time it took us to get home, that the moment for discipline had come. He thought he was being saved by time. When I told him again what was about to happen and why, I could see his little mind working to find an escape and then he just looked up at me with tender eyes and said, "But I'm just a little guy."

Without maturity, we naturally look for a simple way out without learning or even repenting. It is uncanny the ability of humanity to ignore the reality of consequence. In the case of parents and children, it falls to the parents to exercise good judgment. It sounds like a paradox but this is the ground where there can be peace and war when good ideas confront bad ones.

When my son treats his mother with disrespect, she must make peace with the need to bring teaching and correction to the circumstance. If she does not, then that is the way he will treat his wife and that is the way his children will treat their mother. A lack of action hurts many and ultimately destroys peace where a decisive action creates only a moment of frustration but eventually leads to peace.

Seeing a problem calls for an educated reaction to it. We cannot look the other way. Doesn't God see our heart when we see a wrong that is within our responsible reach and doesn't He see how we react?

Wanting peace does not mean we don't make war. We choose the fight that is right. It is not that we are out for a fight, but that we are intent on being whatever God needs us to be in any given circumstance. To hunger and thirst after righteousness is to profoundly desire to do what is right in any given circumstance. There is a time to confront and a time to let be. There is a time to release and a time to try again and the answer is not always the same. When a drug addict is responding to Jesus and trying to get clean, it might not be the best time to drill them about junk food.

I Like a Good Fight

Fight the good fight of the faith. Take hold of the eternal life to which you were called when you made your good confession in the presence of many witnesses.

1 Timothy 6:12 NIV

Being a man of peace does not mean I turn the other way during conflict. In fact, sometimes it means just the opposite. Don't confuse meekness with insecurity. When I recognize unwitting error, I don't just smile and close my eyes saying, "This is just what the immature do."

Jesus was quick to rebuke His disciples when their thinking was erroneous. Paul certainly took time to deal with inconsistencies. The goal is educated response.

Sometimes doing the right thing will cause a separation. Jesus came to give choice; to lead us to a crossroad. It is the good fight of faith in the individual that causes us to stand with some things and choose not to stand with others.

> *Let us hold fast the profession of our faith without wavering;*
> *(for he is faithful that promised;) And let us consider one*
> *another to provoke unto love and to good works.*
>
> *Hebrews 10:23-24 KJV*

"The Faith" is a phrase that does not describe a single act of confidence, but rather a phrase that embodies the entirety of what Christianity represents. Jesus came as one who would bring peace to all people (Luke 2:14), but He did also lift up a whip and clear the temple when it became a money market for the clever and not a refuge for the weak. There are attitudes that should never be found coexisting.

> *For the son dishonoureth the father, the daughter riseth up*
> *against her mother, the daughter in law against her mother*
> *in law; a man's enemies are the men of his own house.*
>
> *Micah 7:6 KJV*

These scriptures paint a picture of the effect of God's Word in the lives of those who would either accept it or reject it. I cannot always control having peace with others as they also have to make a choice.

> *If it is possible, as far as it depends on you, live at peace with*
> *everyone.*
>
> *Romans 12:18 NIV*

Life Discovery

Peace in the Storm

A realistic view of our world shows plainly that some people do not want peace. But like David said,

Thou preparest a table before me in the presence of mine enemies: thou anointest my head with oil; my cup runneth over.

Psalm 23:5 KJV

What an odd picture David paints of peace in the midst of hostility. This tranquility is the fruit of staying true to God no matter what. This is a picture of a heart that is committed to God's way. The Bible is full of stories of how faithful men and women stood by their testimony even when the outward world was more than hostile towards them because of their faith.

Shadrach, Meshach, and Abed-Nego answered and said to the king, "O Nebuchadnezzar, we have no need to answer you in this matter. If that is the case, our God whom we serve is able to deliver us from the burning fiery furnace, and He will deliver us from your hand, O king. But if not, let it be known to you, O king, that we do not serve your gods, nor will we worship the gold image which you have set up."

Daniel 3:16-18

We do live in a faithless world, but that does not mean we lose our faith and our convictions. We can make peace with what is right and rest in the midst of storms (Deuteronomy 33:12, Mark 4:38). It is in the quiet place of our hearts that we choose to honor the Lord above all else and make no peace with the enemy.

Making Peace

Don't team up with those who are unbelievers. How can righteousness be a partner with wickedness? How can light live with darkness? What harmony can there be between Christ and the devil? How can a believer be a partner with an unbeliever? And what union can there be between God's temple and idols? For we are the temple of the living God. As God said: "I will live in them and walk among them. I will be their God, and they will be my people. Therefore, "Come out from among unbelievers and separate yourselves from them, says the LORD. Don't touch their filthy things, and I will welcome you. And I will be your Father, and you will be my sons and daughters."

2 Corinthians 6:14-18 NLT

Too often the world around us tells us what to love, what to hate and even who to be. We measure up to the standard of those looking down on us or we are outcast, all with winks, smiles and pats on the back. This produces feelings of profound frustration as we pass through life unhappy, filled with the despair of inadequacy or not measuring up to.....them.

The Key to Peace

There are inclinations written deep within our being that help us to regain our footing if we can but listen to God's voice and exercise the confidence to follow. God's leading can be quite clear through convictions that are defined by Scripture. There is an inner voice that grows out of increased knowledge. You might even understand it as a gut feeling that becomes stronger with Christian maturity. It is an ability placed within us by God to interact with spiritual truth. This spiritual cooperation will lead us to peace if we will follow.

These inward feelings are fueled and affirmed by the Holy Scriptures. The keys or ideals of the Kingdom, which are hidden in Christ, are a most precious treasure. Biblical ideals are what will put us back on track. It is seeing in the Bible God's passionate desire to teach us, to restore us and even to be with us that will give us the confidence to begin acting on our insights that have agreement with God's Word. Jesus, who is God's very Word become flesh, is the key to making peace.

> *Peace I leave with you, my peace I give unto you: not as the world giveth, give I unto you. Let not your heart be troubled, neither let it be afraid.*
>
> *John 14:27 KJV*

God is ever leading us to peace with the gentle breeze of His voice. This intuitive knowledge will lead us to what is right, leading us away from what is wrong and then we can be baptized into the full knowledge of experience with God's Word. Doing what we hear from the Bible is what will help us embrace truth that is sometimes very different from the voices of those that would manipulate us for their own ends.

Voices of manipulation are not always hostile with evil intent and can even be very sincere and well intentioned, as in the case of Peter trying to protect Jesus in Matthew chapter 16. In the end though, whatever asks us to deny our own convictions and embrace another's is dangerous. It is an enemy and a stumbling block. Never surrender your own responsibility to follow your own convictions.

The Great Crossroad

Real peace can be found as we trust what God has made us to be. Through the knowledge of God, we see the face of Jesus and

Making Peace

that image emerges as the very image of God and the very revelation of ourselves. Seeing ourselves in Him helps us make sense of the internal searching and spiritual hunger that is driving us and it will also help us to distinguish with confidence what is good from what is bad. This is the great crossroad; deciding what place we allow God and His knowledge to hold in our lives.

> *My son, if you accept my words and store up my commands within you, turning your ear to wisdom and applying your heart to understanding, and if you call out for insight and cry aloud for understanding, and if you look for it as for silver and search for it as for hidden treasure, then you will understand the fear of the LORD and find the knowledge of God.*
>
> *Proverbs 2:1-5 NIV*

Adding Value to Life

Through the interaction of Biblical knowledge and obedient experience, we begin to unlock and even understand our feelings and ambitions. Much of what we want is born of good desire needing only the rudder of God's Word to make the course both sure and productive. This is the beginning of making peace with ourselves.

"It is a journey that is neither rushed nor detoured," as my grandmother used to say, if we keep our mind stayed on Him. This journey of life discovery will always push us on as the light of God's Word is heeded. It adds line upon line of knowledge as step after step is securely taken. Godly principle will be added to previous principles that will continue to add increased value to life. What lives will continue to sink its roots deep into the soil of good ground to ever strengthen its new growth.

Life Discovery

All life is precious, of course, but unrealized value is not the same thing as accessible worth. We have great potential and we have all seen some life wasted. Adding value to life ultimately rests in the knowledge of God realized in the individual.

The love I had for my wife five years ago was wonderful but today it is so much richer, so much….better. We now have a deeper meeting of the minds. There was so much we needed to learn about each other, especially since we came from different countries, from different cultures. We have been married for 20 years now and though I have been so happy with her for all these years, there has always been an ever present need for greater awareness.

Progressing in Knowledge

If the principles that govern our decisions are defined by the Bible and the life of Jesus, then we are sure to have a peace that is beyond the normal parameters of our understanding. Jesus emerges as the measure of life and the measure of peace.

> *Don't worry about anything; instead, pray about everything. Tell God what you need, and thank him for all he has done. Then you will experience God's peace, which exceeds anything we can understand. His peace will guard your hearts and minds as you live in Christ Jesus.*
>
> *Philippians 4:6-7 NLT*

My wife was born in a different country than I was and her first language is different than mine, but beyond these superficial cultural differences, we are two unique sovereign beings. The language and the cultural difference made the road we walked a bit longer, but in the end, we were just two people who had to learn how to understand each other. This is the same dynamic between us and God. We are learning a new language, a new culture.

Making Peace

We learn to understand Him as we learn to understand each other and even ourselves. My wife and I both had unique definitions of marriage and expectations in life. I am learning a new language in life as I learn to communicate as a person to her. I am learning her language. She uses words that are associated with feelings and experiences quite different than mine. That does not make one of us wrong but it does mean both of us need to learn.

Language is something that grows with experience. If a word does not have an experience it can call on, then it does not have lasting meaning. What if a word does not mean the same to you as it does to another? Making peace is the journey of learning and accepting new ideas or even adding to ideas that you already have. God is so much more than we ever knew or understood but through the Bible, He shares words with us that are defined by the life of Jesus and by others in the great cloud of witnesses. Language becomes the gateway to life and peace.

Making Peace Through Language

My six year old asked why our dogs couldn't talk and I told him that God didn't make them to talk. He did design us to talk though. Dogs don't need to talk but we do. It's more than a desire. It is a need that is both fundamental and profound.

We all are learning different levels of the use of language and knowledge. This is how we interact with our world. We are built to discover. We are designed to communicate and language is the tool as it captures feelings and experiences along with emotions and it makes them transferable.

Some value communication more than others. We all use communication for different reasons. Some exercise greater intention with this powerful tool.

Death and life are in the power of the tongue, And those who love it will eat its fruit.

Proverbs 18:21

When I first tried to use my wife's language to express to her my feelings of love it felt very insincere. Not only was I inexperienced in love but I was unfamiliar with the words of love. Though my words eventually became correct, my experience with those words in her language was superficial at best. Nonetheless, I had to begin that journey of real communication if we were to grow together in life. The way we expressed love in the beginning was well intentioned but it is so much richer today as we have learned each other's language and built around it a world of experiences.

Thinking about the journey I have had with my wife makes me think of the journey I now have with God and with myself and even with people. I am ever learning a new culture in the lives of those I meet.

Making peace with God in the beginning feels strange because we begin to use a language that is unfamiliar to us. It is a new language. There are phrases such as, "I can do all things through Christ who strengthens me." These words sound nice but it's not until they are experienced that they begin to have meaning and even authority. Even as our words become correct, it is not until we associate the words with experience that they become life changing; even life giving.

God has expressed love to us so many times, but it is difficult for us to comprehend and accept His unfailing, unconditional love until we have realized it; experienced it and accepted it.

Making Peace

Having peace with God is not just communicating with Him but also letting Him communicate with us and allowing that sharing of information to affect the way life is approached.

The way that we use the name of Jesus in the beginning is a kind of historical recognition or maybe even a vague awareness of His presence, but in the process of time, that name comes to mean more than the definition of God; it grows into meaning the presence of God. The name of Jesus becomes even the approval and the endorsement of God in life's activities. That name becomes a defining point of how we approach God and how He relates to us. At some point, we discover God with us and the name Immanuel takes on a new feel.

The Journey of Knowledge

Beginning on this road of discovery is glorious but continuing on this road of learning and obedience is what takes us to the promised land of real peace in life. Even just a beginning level of Biblical knowledge is a great encouragement because it means that the journey of peace has already begun.

There was a great thinker who said that there really are not different kinds of love but rather deeper levels of love. We allow ourselves to feel a deeper love for a friend than a stranger, but there is a much deeper love we feel for a spouse. Imagine the level of love we allow ourselves to feel towards the child of a friend as opposed to our own child? It is in an ever developing circumstantial awareness of love, sacrifice, responsibility and commitment that we gain as we progress or regress in life depending on the governing principles that direct the nature of our relations.

Maturity and experience enlarges, our feelings of commitment to those beyond our immediate world. This does not create distance between those close to us, but rather brings closer those who are further away. These are not different kinds of love but rather deeper levels of love allowed, experienced and understood.

How wonderful it is once we have discovered Jesus to realize He is a reflection of our very own soul; like deep water that ever allows deeper penetration.

The better developed languages often have several words that describe single ideas such as love or anger, knowledge or even maturity. It's not that there are always different things being defined by different words, but rather different words that describe a variety of associations with the same thing. Words simply describe experiences and allow us to share these experiences with others. Some experiences are more profound than others.

Making Peace with Self

God is helping us to discover truth that leads us in life, leading us to peace. Discovering ourselves in Jesus and making peace with who we are is one of the greatest moments we will ever experience. We are always the same people, but at every season of growth, we see more of Jesus, we see more of ourselves and we become more settled. Once you make peace with being Christ-like, you find a wonderful beginning. I want to be more than what I am right now, but right now, I am! What a wonderful peace indeed.

In God's scheme, the purest love is a love given without obligation; a love that says, "I love you because you are a part of humanity, not because I can get something from you. If you don't respond to my love, I still feel the same way about you."

As individuals, we should be the first partakers of real peace but sometimes it's difficult to forgive one's own self. It can be complicated to love ourselves with that unconditional kind of commitment when we fall short of our own expectations. Too often we place limitations on ourselves because we don't feel worthy to reach up, to look up.

We are surrounded with so many conflicting voices of what the definition of peace really is. These ideas profoundly affect the way we look at ourselves. Again, it is a variety of voices that are seeding us and each one is trying to win our affection, if not our loyalty. Imagine the humility of God to place His voice in the middle of so many other voices, but He did. He really does believe in us.

It is natural for us to love because we are the children of God and He is love, but the boundaries and the focus of love differ so greatly from person to person and from culture to culture because of the variety of ways that people experience and express love.

Cultures torn by war will show love in one way, while cultures filled with wealth and peace will express it in another way. In one place, it is bravery that is admired while in another, advancement by any means is what is coveted. One culture honors entertainment while another honors loyalty and the next praises wealth. The distinct definitions of love are understandable but still God has provided for us a clearer and more thorough definition of love through Jesus. Knowing what God loves is discovering the heart of peace.

The Only True Definition

We must embrace God as the standard if we are to experience true peace. As we learn to trust God more, we fear man less and it becomes easier to move into deep, still waters of peace. Here we can experience true calm as we let God teach us about life. Living at peace allows us to trust in these new wings of love that will carry us right up to the frontier of the limitless world of Christian living. This is where the conflict ends and the peace begins. As we find peace with God, we discover peace with ourselves and with others.

As experiences or even the need for an experience arises in our heart, we all react differently. People all over the world are passionately serving some idea of god in so many different ways. Moslems, like Buddhists and Hindus, are dedicated to their religion because it is a basic human need to express spirituality, to experience spirituality, to embrace some degree of faith.

Religions agree on the existence of a higher power, but it is only Jesus who can bring peace into the heart by defining for us who God really is, who we really are, what He wants to do for us and what He wants to receive from us. God, through Jesus, is defining our expectations of religion and of man and ourselves.

Jesus is the only true definition of God and of life and of peace. He is the true reflection of what we are destined to be and how we should shape the world around us. We make peace with ourselves only as we make peace with the reality that seeing Jesus is seeing God and that's the same as seeing ourselves.

I have discovered Real Power

CHOOSE THIS DAY

*C*hoosing to recognize and react to the circumstances that constantly surround you each day in a Christian way flows from recognizing the tremendous eternal consequences that are inseparably attached to each decision. Daily choices are important. Good choices flow from good character and good character in choice represents, among other things, the consistent moral reaction to situations regardless of fatigue or pressure. Each day, we must face whatever crosses our path in the light of Jesus' name.

> *Take therefore no thought for the morrow: for the morrow shall take thought for the things of itself. Sufficient unto the day is the evil thereof.*
>
> *Matthew 6:34 KJV*

This entails not just confronting the circumstances of today, but confronting the circumstances of today in the name of Jesus. That's the same as saying that Jesus and His definition of life must truly be Lord of every decision. What a fantastic discipline that we strive for; considering Jesus in everything that we think, say and do!

Life Discovery

And whatsoever ye do in word or deed, do all in the name of the Lord Jesus, giving thanks to God and the Father by him.

Colossians 3:17 KJV

Choosing today is not a thing to be feared, as some might fear making a bad decision, but choosing is a thing to be respected and even revered as we learn to consider the Lord in all we do. The leading of God is ever with us to give us courage and confidence. Even when we might make an impulsive or even a bad decision, the Lord is ever with us to help us quickly back on course.

Be strong and courageous. Do not be afraid or terrified because of them, for the LORD your God goes with you; he will never leave you nor forsake you.

Deuteronomy 31:6 NIV

It's Not Something We Lose

Faith in God in the midst of life's daily practice is not something we lose, but it is something that we often fail to consider. God will not leave us alone to make errors, but often we push ahead into things without taking time to pray and consider what God wants, even though we are deeply aware of an internal hesitation. Too often we press on against our own counsel.

A man's own folly ruins his life, yet his heart rages against the LORD.

Proverbs 19:3 NIV

Twenty/tewenty hindsight does not help us avoid damage already done through harsh words or impetuous decisions. It does not take a lot of wisdom to look back and sigh as regrets are gathered and filed neatly with other past failures. But to look ahead prayerfully!

Choose This Day

The wise are cautious and avoid danger; fools plunge ahead with reckless confidence.

Proverbs 14:16 NLT

Good choices can be made by everyone when they are influenced by godly knowledge and wisdom. There will always be unforeseen elements around us because people will almost always be involved in the world around us, but the fact remains that the majority of circumstances can be observed before they come to fruition.

I Want to Be a Millionaire

A new acquaintance of mine made an effort to get me to invest in an oil well that was a "sure thing." I had literally just met the man having spent just one afternoon with him. He wanted me to exercise my influence within my own world of friends to put together a quite large sum of money in the name of nothing less than supporting Christian efforts. Wow! What a great opportunity. Choices needed to be made.

My first logical thought as I stared intently at his nice smile was that I knew nothing about the oil business. I mean, nothing other than filling my car with gas and keeping my machines maintained. I'm not even sure if gas comes out of oil or if it comes out of something else.

My second thought was that in the very short time I knew this man, I really knew nothing of consequence about him. He was a stranger to me just yesterday morning and today I found myself the beneficiary of our profound friendship.

My third thought was what made me cringe. By offering this deal to my friends, I was not only being irresponsible with my own reputation but I would become the facilitator of danger in their lives through my own naivety. How could I ask people to take risk on my word about something that I had already realized I knew nothing about and with someone I hardly knew?

Of course there were also internal red flags, a still small voice within gave me pause, but right now I am simply talking about logical, godly foresight. Let's safely assume that if God had spoken to me and made His will known to me that I would have been pleased to pursue this great venture, but that was not the case here. I was left only with my mind.

I sat there and smiled the man as I considered how nicely his smile framed those pearly white teeth. It was like being in a movie and I sort of enjoyed it. I was the object of a real scam. Deeper down I wondered why I looked like a target but that was a question for later consideration.

Tragedy and scandal were right there within arm's reach, but that enemy floated harmlessly by because of an educated choice in a circumstance that lacked education. I knew what I did not know, so knowledge won the day over ignorance. Knowledge led the way on to surer paths and kept me away from optimistic presumption….I mean, wishful thinking. At the very least, I knew I needed educated counsel.

Foresight Awareness

In other scenarios, you might find yourself in the company of a gossiping, backbiting and accusing person. Simple awareness will take note of what is obvious. You should never be surprised if a person like this eventually turns on you. Recognizing the obvious will allow simple parameters to be set that can protect from needless offenses and betrayals.

Foresight and awareness are powerful tools for the person who is proactive in his world and practiced in the presence of God. By foresight, I mean acknowledging the obvious as it comes, not after it goes by. By awareness, I refer to the constant oversight of Christian morals as decisions are weighed.

> But strong meat belongeth to them that are of full age, even those who by reason of use have their senses exercised to discern both good and evil.
>
> Hebrews 5:14 KJV

We are talking about choosing this day, today, right now; facing today the decisions that lie right in front of you. Today we choose what to react to and how to react to it. Choices that are forced without proper evaluation are dangerous as a rule. Avoiding rash and quick judgments is safe and it keeps us within the boundaries of appropriate reaction.

> Understand this, my dear brothers and sisters: You must all be quick to listen, slow to speak, and slow to get angry.
>
> James 1:19 NLT

We lose control of our lives when we lose control of our decisions; allowing the foolishness of ourselves or of others to dictate how we ourselves decide.

Choosing for Yourself

The process of making a good choice includes the gathering of information and the pursuit of wise counsel, but at the end of the road, each person chooses for themselves what they will do and allow and each person lives with the results. We can never hand off our own responsibility to exercise good choice skills. God commanded each one of us as individuals to choose in life what we will follow and serve.

> *"Today I have given you the choice between life and death, between blessings and curses. Now I call on heaven and earth to witness the choice you make. Oh, that you would choose life, so that you and your descendants might live!*
>
> *Deuteronomy 30:19 NLT*

This was not Moses choosing for the people but it was Moses presenting a choice to the people. I am sure if he could have made this decision for them, he would have. If Jesus could have made this decision for us, He would have but He limited Himself by giving us the power to choose. He said, "Call on Me and you will be saved."

It would have only been greed and lust that would have pushed me forward with the oil well partnership, as sound reason would have never allowed such an ignorant pursuit. (Ignorance being the lack of knowledge). It will always be a good indicator of a bad decision when principles, counsels and patience are not allowed to vote. Have you ever tried to hide your decisions from others you really should have considered? Recognize those witty impulses to push you through the gate too quickly where wisdom cries out.

Choose Godly Consequence

God created us all with a fantastic intellect that is remarkably capable. We have eyes that see the world around us with all of its beauty, with all of its wonder and we have a mind that can assimilate the information passed through the eye. It is after seeing that we set the boundaries and definitions of the judgments that will carve into our world the character of our own being. Our minds give us power to choose today - the power to choose godly consequence over godless consequence.

Consequence is not just a negative result of bad decisions but it is also the rewarding fruit of good decisions. Marriage can be wonderful. Children can be a blessing and church can be a great place to be. These fruits, whether good or bad, flow from our moments of decision. Choosing well does not mean each moment is comfortable, but it does mean that life in the big picture is healthy even as we journey through difficult terrain while we cross the natural divide into eternity.

The Real Decision

Therefore doth my Father love me, because I lay down my life, that I might take it again. No man taketh it from me, but I lay it down of myself. I have power to lay it down, and I have power to take it again.

John 10:17-18 KJV

Jesus made the decision to lay His life down. No one took His life from Him. He gave it; His life as a ransom for many. Consequence to Him was not the rolling of the dice. He knew the power of His choice and He made the decision to pay for our sin on the cross willingly.

We, too, face a similar crossroad as we decide what we will give our lives for. Embracing Christianity brings a whole new dimension to priorities. This light directs us to face the real decision of what we will hunger and thirst after.

I have set you an example that you should do as I have done for you.

John 13:15 NIV

Calculated Results

Consequence is a calculated result when embraced with fore-sight, and foresight to the Christian is firmly established in God's Word. This makes consequence a predetermined result to the one who believes. This is real vision, like when God spoke knowing that His Word would prosper in what it was sent to accomplish.

So shall my word be that goeth forth out of my mouth: it shall not return unto me void, but it shall accomplish that which I please, and it shall prosper in the thing whereto I sent it.

Isaiah 55:11 KJV

Real vision does not just know where you are going, but it is realizing where you are and then embracing God in the process of the choices that will mark the way. We are not out of control of our lives, being tossed about by the reckless hands of random fate. We choose each day; indeed we choose this day what voice will guide us and what object will benefit from our love and strength. Far from being out of control, we are in fact instrumentally in control of the world around us by the decisions that we make each day.

Think about this. In death, there is an act of dying and then there is the consequence of dying which carries a soul into an everlasting reckoning. You could say this is a picture of the first and the second death. This eternal consequence is fed by the umbilical cord of choices.

Living is the same. There is a moment when life is conceived and then birthed into this world. This is the first birth. Then there is the consequence of receiving Jesus, the second birth or being born again. The decision to be born again carries also a life consequence, which is filled with the life of God and His influence along with it.

God formed in each one of us a sovereign will or an individual ability to choose what will be reached for in life and then He determined that each would reap the simple fruit of his own wisdom's seed. No, we are not rolling the dice in life but we are choosing each day the path to life or the broad road that leads to death. We choose what we allow our minds to dwell on, just like we choose to say the things that we say.

At each realization every day we choose the quality of the moral fiber we weave into the moment. Eventually our choices are then shown to be just or revealed to be evil by the eternal fruit that passes plainly in front of the eyes of God who consistently weighs the heart where true motivations are stored. It is our destiny to choose and ironically, we have no choice but to choose. Realizing this is the first step in harnessing the wonderful power of decision.

The sun did set on that blessed day
and new hope did fill his mind

DEFINING DECISIONS

I was at a football game my son was playing in and I rose to my feet with the rest of the crowd as we all prepared to sing the national anthem of the United States. Marching onto the field were three older gentlemen who, with flags flying and shoulders erect, moved together in a proud march to their appointed place. Collectively they stood and saluted the flag of our country.

There was a reverence about them that filled the stadium with silence. There was something about these guys that gave us all pause. These were men who believed in their country. The flag they carried was somehow different than other flags. It was their flag and it seemed to carry in it the very convictions of their hearts if not the deeds of their days.

It was evident that these men really believed. They fought for what they believed in. Their ideals drove them to do incredible things despite their fear, and it was their convictions that launched them into the furious unknown even though their lives were surly in the balance. There was a freedom and a courage in them that dictated their actions. We could all feel it. We could see it. It was inspirational in a way that called you to be a better person.

Life Discovery

Where did this freedom and courage we saw in them come from? At some point in their lives, something defined these character traits for them and in them. Someone influenced them to have this kind of attitude, their view of right and wrong, their ethical system of acceptable and unacceptable behavior and how to react to the contrary. At some point, they framed their ideals about the nature and the boundaries of responsibility, freedom and morality.

As those thoughts continued to roll through my mind, I became a bit emotional as that great marching band began to play and the national anthem rang out shamelessly into the atmosphere. The three veterans saluted with unwavering focus. "Freedom" and "courage" were the words that flooded my mind and triggered this rush of feelings. These were precious words; costly ideals.

Those three retired soldiers were dressed in badly outdated clothing but what pride they carried with their presence. It was a pride that irrevocably upheld their defined principles; principles of being our brother's keeper, by duty, by sacrifice.

Diversity

I wondered for a minute about how others in this stadium were being affected by this scene that had so gripped me. Everyone was quiet and respectful but as I began to look across the crowd that day, I began to see how diverse these people really were.

I was on the verge of an epiphany. Those old soldiers triggered in me a great soul searching but as I looked around, I almost got the feeling that I was the only one in this state of mind.

There were different people, different minds and different realities. There were different nationalities present and different religions. There were those who were immoral and those who were devout; those who ate and those who played. There were so many different guidelines to life in this one stadium, in this single moment.

There were teenagers flirting and adolescents with a look of escaping in their eyes. There were grandparents, parents and college students mingled in with the blue collar workers who sat not far from the white collar representation.

Imagine how many diverse ways this medley of people would view family, discipline, education, money and respect. How many different ways could this group define courage and freedom? How many different ways could they define God, faith and obligation?

I smile now as I write about this thought provoking scene. The fact is that I did not even know the men who were at this point singing the national anthem. It is possible that they were immoral and bitter old men, but I was still projecting my own beliefs about what I thought a noble man would be. It still holds true that these projected ideals of mine about freedom and courage are the ideals that I am reaching for and they were formed in me at some point by some experience.

Knowing the Source

As we reach for definitions in life, we all choose the source of those definitions. The source could be derived from family, experience, culture or even friends. Something wrote your law. It could have been your dazzling intellect or your lazy heart. Some people are too lazy to think or even too lazy to react, while others know no restraint. The fact is that we all have an image we are reaching for and something authored that image.

We have all been formed in some environment that defined us such as a religious home or a party house. It could have been a family caught in the cruel jaws of divorce that shaped your attitude or it could have been a loving family that helped you define your expectations. Every country and every culture has such a wide variety of definitions.

God sent His Word to us so that we could know the true definition of human expectation written down by the one and only Author of Life. Some people ignore Him and shipwreck their lives. Others embrace Him and in so doing, add immeasurable value to life. The Bible is the right definition of life. It is the one definition that works eternally. Just another reason it is called the Gospel or the Good News.

The Good News

Thy words were found, and I did eat them; and thy word was unto me the joy and rejoicing of mine heart: for I am called by thy name, O LORD God of hosts.

Jeremiah 15:16 KJV

When the Bible talks about the Gospel, it does not just say, "the Gospel." It says the Gospel of Jesus Christ. "Gospel" simply means good news. When a baby is born, it is good news or the gospel of a birth. When a special gift is given, it is good news or gospel. When you hear your favorite team wins their game, it is good news or we could say gospel. There are many gospels in life that are wonderful to experience on many different levels but when the word is clearly defined as the Gospel of Jesus Christ, it means something much more potent than a simple good news report.

Defining Decisions

The Gospel of Jesus Christ means there is good news that we are forgiven, we are saved from eternal sin and death, we are also healed in our spirit, soul, and body and most importantly, we can once again have an active and vital relationship with God. The Gospel of Jesus Christ is the greatest news that will ever reach our ears.

Let's look at this good news in another way. Remember, it is the good news of Jesus Christ. "Jesus" is His name and "Christ" defines the kind of relationship we have with Him. This is a very specific kind of good news.

Look at it this way. Daddy is not my name, it is a title or you could say it describes the kind of relationship I have with specific children; my children. Policeman is not a name, it is a title that describes the specific nature of the relationship intended. A policeman does not come in his own name because he does not represent himself. He represents the law of the government. The title attached to a name defines the experience we have with that particular person.

Jesus came as the Christ of God. This title "Christ" communicates the specific nature of the relationship intended by God. Jesus is His specific name and Christ describes the relationship we have with that historical person. He is the Savior of the world; the only Savior.

Neither is there salvation in any other: for there is none other name under heaven given among men, whereby we must be saved.

Acts 4:12 KJV

Life Discovery

I, even I, am the LORD; and beside me there is no savior.

Isaiah 43:11 KJV

The Gospel of Jesus Christ is the very power of God unto salvation to those that believe it (Romans 1:16)! To the rest of humanity, there is left no other salvation. Accepting the Good News of Jesus Christ is embracing God's desire to restore your life through Jesus. That is a very different piece of good news from the news that says we have a new car. The Word of God is truly powerful. How can we compare it to any wisdom or ideal of man's making?

For my thoughts are not your thoughts, neither are your ways my ways, saith the LORD. For as the heavens are higher than the earth, so are my ways higher than your ways, and my thoughts than your thoughts.

Isaiah 55:8-9 KJV

Measured by Definition

Remember that the word "Gospel" to the one who got a new car is not as powerful as the word "Gospel" to the one who has just been released from eternal damnation. As we look at the power of definition, consider words like "freedom" and "courage." The way a veteran would relate to these words is very different than the way John Lennon would define these words. The use of these words could relay such a wide variety of meanings and associative perspectives. One could say, "I'm free!" after getting through a difficult exam and another could say, "I'm free!" after being released from prison. Essentially the word means the same thing, but the level of life changing influence is a world apart.

A Christian could say, "I'm free from sin and eternal death!" after having an experience with God and another person could

Defining Decisions

say, "I am free from my house payment!" after having made his last mortgage payment. Both are happy, but what a world of difference there is in the result of each freedom. When God is allowed to begin defining our words and choices then what a powerful difference it makes.

The word "love" is shallow to a teenager talking about his iPod but imagine the life change when this same teenager begins to understand love as God defines it. Imagine the change that is introduced into his life when God's love begins to influence his concepts of forgiveness, sacrifice and responsibility. The power is in the definition.

Some might say, "I am free to sin" and they would be right. Another might define the same freedom as the power to follow God. What power there is in definition! The same word can carry you the distance between heaven and hell. How many different definitions could we find for freedom if we asked an Indian or an African or an Italian? What if we asked an old citizen of China as opposed to a teenager in China today how they each define freedom? How would a Charismatic Christian define freedom and how would it differ from a traditional Christian? What about an ex-con or an old drug addict? So many definitions!

Some hopes are good while some hopes are not. It is the quality of these hopes, or should we say the quality of what defines these hopes, that determines their eternal value. Power is in the definition.

Capsules of Our Lives

The depth of influence of freedom and courage is fueled by the ideals and convictions, that support them. Within our personal standards and convictions we nurture our truest intention. There are many today who use the words "freedom" and "courage" to flaunt immorality and appetite while there are others who use freedom and courage to tear free from the corruption that is in the world. The fact is that the words themselves carry nothing more than the power of the believer's definition. It's not the word that is magic, but it is the faith that empowers the word that ignites it.

Defining our choices means defining our convictions. What we believe is what eventually comes out. What we have in our hearts will eventually rule in our lives.

> *For as he thinketh in his heart, so is he.*
>
> *Proverbs 23:7 KJV*

By defining our convictions, we choose what each word in life means to us such as marriage, parenthood, loyalty, judgment, responsibility, faith, hope, love and so many more. Each word we use carries a little piece of us with it. Words become little capsules of our lives. Defining convictions is the exercise in defining the words that we know and use. This practice should be deliberate.

We decide what is right and what is wrong for ourselves. We decide what we will settle for and what will never measure up. We decide how we influence people and who we allow to influence us.

Meet the Governor

As Christians, by definition, we are disciples of Christ. Jesus is our functioning Lord. That technically means Jesus governs our lives. He is the author of life and it is He who is training us, leading us by word and example how we must confront the myriad of circumstances that cross our path each day.

Defining Decisions

By confessing Jesus as Lord, we have been allowed into the Kingdom of God where His will is done on earth through us as it is in heaven. Our part in God's kingdom brings a very sober light into the process of defining our convictions. As humans, we each reflect our own wisdom onto the world and as Christians, we reflect Him.

Governing Ourselves

Intentionally representing the Kingdom of God is the discipline of a true disciple. Since the way we think directs the way we both speak and act, then laboring to govern the way we think is the first frontier to be crossed as we enter into the Kingdom of God and accept the role of representative.

The Bible actually teaches that we should bring every thought into captivity and measure it up against the knowledge of Christ. Since actions flow from our thoughts, this becomes an indispensable exercise.

> *For though we walk in the flesh, we do not war after the flesh: (For the weapons of our warfare are not carnal, but mighty through God to the pulling down of strong holds;) Casting down imaginations, and every high thing that exalteth itself against the knowledge of God, and bringing into captivity every thought to the obedience of Christ;*
>
> *2 Corinthians 10:3-5 KJV*

Thoughts include ambitions, fears, desires, judgments and whatever else enters the arena of our mind. It's more than just the ideas we ponder but deeper, it reflects the emotions we allow to be attached to each idea. These thoughts and feelings must be brought to the feet of Jesus and properly defined or they can become the very seeds of our demise.

As Christians, it is knowledge that directs our decisions; specifically the knowledge of Christ which is God's way to save us, to lead us. Defining our true convictions begins here deliberately. It is within the ideas we have about Him that we discover power in life to do and to be. God defined life through Jesus and now we choose the level of influence we allow Jesus and His Word to have in our lives. Seeing life through the eyes of Jesus is the only true and lasting source of life definition and consequently, the only true and lasting peace to be found is wrapped up in Him.

> *I want them to have complete confidence that they understand God's mysterious plan, which is Christ himself. In him lie hidden all the treasures of wisdom and knowledge.*
>
> *Colossians 2:2-3 NLT*

The Narrow Road

Choosing to let God define the way we react instead of letting the world dictate appropriate responses brings us to the great divide. This is the place where we determine what exactly is the knowledge that directs our choices today, whether it be God or the world. Will we choose the narrow road of God's ideas or take the broad road that leads to destruction?

> *"You can enter God's Kingdom only through the narrow gate. The highway to hell is broad, and its gate is wide for the many who choose that way. But the gateway to life is very narrow, and the road is difficult, and only a few ever find it.*
>
> *Matthew 7:13-14 NLT*

Defining Decisions

It seems overly simplistic to ask someone if they want to choose life or death, but it has evolved into one of the most crucial and misunderstood decisions in human history. This is the question that built the platform on which original sin played itself out. Why are the waters of decision so difficult to navigate even when all of the information is readily at hand?

People are still overeating, smoking and doing drugs even though there are endless resources of both books and real life testimonies about the results. These facts are common knowledge, not obscure bits of information yet thousands each day pull up a chair to these tables to play a hand thinking somehow they will be the lucky ones. It's amazing the ability of a human to ignore consequence.

The need for freedom and the courage to act becomes a viciously deadly snare without the rudder of God's knowledge.

Blinded by the Dark

Kept by erroneous definitions, confusion and ignorance, humanity is driven to respond to their natural desires without the light of God's Word to direct their path.

> *Satan, who is the god of this world, has blinded the minds of those who don't believe. They are unable to see the glorious light of the Good News. They don't understand this message about the glory of Christ, who is the exact likeness of God.*
> *2 Corinthians 4:4 NLT*

Incongruously, those who are blinded by the dark labor to fortify their positions against assault and even run from the light. Trying to protect their lives, they move further into the shadows where only shame and suffering abide. Strongholds are built to protect from unwanted intrusion and danger and it is these strongholds that ironically become the prisons of despair.

> *The weapons we fight with are not the weapons of the world. On the contrary, they have divine power to demolish strongholds.*
>
> *2 Corinthians 10:4 NIV*

Let's make something clear as a matter of definition, cigarette addiction is not a stronghold but should be defined as a bad habit. A stronghold is better viewed as the ideals we have built in our own minds that we think are keeping us safe.

These standards are fortified with social agreement, university backing, family expectations and personal conviction. These are thoughts that are ever feeding off the preferred environment we choose to mingle with. We listen to the words that voice agreement and we fight against the words that get close enough to challenge.

To be blinded by the dark leads us to hopeless pursuits where nothing can truly satisfy. Even here in the depressing shadows of despair, all we must do to escape is turn the light on. The greatest act of faith is embracing God's word.

The Flower of Faith

> *So then faith cometh by hearing, and hearing by the word of God.*
>
> *Romans 10:17 KJV*

The Bible says that faith comes by hearing. This is the entrance of God's definitions into our process of defining decisions; embracing His ideals. This is where we begin to mingle with heaven's wisdom. God strengthens us as Christians through ideas.

Satan works the same. It is through ideas that he seeks to influence the knowledge that directs our choices. He is the father of lies. Manipulation and distortion are his tools. Confusion is his game.

Ye are of your father the devil, and the lusts of your father ye will do. He was a murderer from the beginning, and abode not in the truth, because there is no truth in him. When he speaketh a lie, he speaketh of his own: for he is a liar, and the father of it.

John 8:44 KJV

Christian faith is the substance of Christian hope or Christ-like ideas. In fact, hope is an idea and it is hope that builds the machine of Christian faith-action.

Now faith is the substance of things hoped for, the evidence of things not seen.

Hebrews 11:1 KJV

Hope is the mental projection of personal expectations that become convictions. This hope begins to spring into life as the flower of faith. Hope governs life as it shapes the decisions that are made. Hope is an idea and it does all this. It is a product of learning. Hope is the fruit of deliberate definition. Definition is the knowledge that we absorb and the quality of that knowledge directly reflects the future. Godly knowledge is our treasure.

Godly Knowledge

Here are just a few verses that show the eternal value of godly knowledge.

The commandments of the LORD are right, bringing joy to

the heart. The commands of the LORD are clear, giving insight for living. Reverence for the LORD is pure, lasting forever. The laws of the LORD are true; each one is fair. They are more desirable than gold, even the finest gold. They are sweeter than honey, even honey dripping from the comb. They are a warning to your servant, a great reward for those who obey them.

Psalm 19:8-11 NLT

How sweet your words taste to me; they are sweeter than honey. Your commandments give me understanding; no wonder I hate every false way of life. Your word is a lamp to guide my feet and a light for my path. I've promised it once, and I'll promise it again: I will obey your righteous regulations.

Psalm 119:103-106 NLT

Wisdom crieth without; she uttereth her voice in the streets: She crieth in the chief place of concourse, in the openings of the gates: in the city she uttereth her words, saying, How long, ye simple ones, will ye love simplicity? and the scorners delight in their scorning, and fools hate knowledge? Turn you at my reproof: behold, I will pour out my spirit unto you, I will make known my words unto you.

Proverbs 1:20-23 KJV

Then they will call to me but I will not answer; they will look for me but will not find me. Since they hated knowledge and did not choose to fear the LORD, since they would not accept my advice and spurned my rebuke, they will eat the fruit of their ways and be filled with the fruit of their schemes.

Proverbs 1:28-31 NIV

Yea, if thou criest after knowledge, and liftest up thy voice for understanding; If thou seekest her as silver, and searchest for her as for hid treasures; Then shalt thou understand the fear of the LORD, and find the knowledge of God. For the LORD giveth wisdom: out of his mouth cometh knowledge and understanding.

Proverbs 2:3-6 KJV

*Now I can see the path that lies before,
surrounded by the sun in all its glory*

IN THE END LIKE THE BEGINNING

*L*ooking at the choices confronted and made by Adam and Eve in the Garden of Eden leads us to the reality that within our very nature, we were designed to make choices. We are supposed to enter into life's soil and choose the path we will follow and we are expected to understand consequences.

We are destined to fall into the ground of this earth and to die to it as we discover a greater life, a new life, an eternal life. Nature itself leads us to the great crossroads of life; the very decisions that will lead us up the narrow road of salvation or down the broad road of destruction.

Nature as well as the cross relentlessly leads us all to our own death, our own final decision where we will reap the consequence of God's life or the thorny harvest of death without God. The life we know now is destined to end one way or the other as it is appointed to each a time to die and then the judgment.

And as it is appointed unto men once to die, but after this the judgment:

Hebrews 9:27 KJV

Life Discovery

The angry nations now get a taste of your anger. The time has come to judge the dead, to reward your servants, all prophets and saints, Reward small and great who fear your Name, and destroy the destroyers of earth.

Revelation 11:18 MSG

We can choose now to lay our lives down willingly or the harsh reality of rejecting God's way will make the decision for us and take our lives from us.

Now think about this: before God created man, before there was sin, before the fall, God created plants, trees, fruits and the like. These were plants created with reproductive seed already within them, already designed to die in the ground before they would ever realize their true destiny (Genesis 1:11-13). These creations carried the invisible things of God within them and they reveal God's design for our lives as sovereign individuals to choose our own master; strangely designed to reproduce only through the powerful tool of final choice which is likened unto death.

Most assuredly, I say to you, unless a grain of wheat falls into the ground and dies, it remains alone; but if it dies, it produces much grain.

John 12:24

You see, a seed must die to realize its destiny. We must choose what we will live for and die for; what will we ultimately give our lives to. This law of life teaches us that God's life is immensely greater and broader than the temporal life we live now.

But as many as received him, to them gave he power to become the sons of God, even to them that believe on his name.

John 1:12 KJV

154

In the End Like the Beginning

What was born of man is destined to live with God (1 John 3:2). Our mortality will be swallowed up in this new life as a shadow is absorbed by the light

O death, where is thy sting? O grave, where is thy victory?
1 Corinthians 15:55 KJV

When God speaks of life, He speaks of much more than life as we know it. His life is not weak with decay. His life has no end. It has no limitations of understanding. Knowing that we are created in His image is being aware of our own immortality, our true spirituality. This eternal nature contained within us as a seed is our destiny.

For whom He foreknew, He also predestined to be conformed
to the image of His Son.
Romans 8:29

Our own eternal interaction with God is the anchor of our soul (Hebrews 6:19), the stability of our temporality. To live life with God's idea of eternity in mind is to find balance and meaning and we are led there as we discover life as God created it, written into our very nature.

Without this eternal perspective, we spend life thinking only of the day, wandering pointlessly, restlessly. Imagine the misery of Solomon to find at the end of every road only temporal vanity or the chasing of the wind (Ecclesiastes 1:14). Often what we give our strength and passion to is nothing more than a flower that fades with the rising of the sun or a mist that vanishes into the air (1 Peter 1:24, James 4:14).

Life Discovery

There is a day of accountability (Romans 14:12). There are eternal consequences (2 Thessalonians 1:8-9, Jude 7). There is a resurrection of the dead (Hebrews 6:2). There is a cross that brings us to relationship with the very power of God (1 Corinthians 1:18). There is a law written into nature that leads us to the law of new life. It grants us true freedom from the darkness and gives us peace with the eternal Word of God. This is Life Discovery.

"God, that we might find freedom through Your Word."

PRAYER OF SALVATION

God loves you—no matter who you are, no matter what your past. God loves you so much that He gave His one and only begotten Son for you. The Bible tells us that "...whoever believes in Him shall not perish but have eternal life" (John 3:16 NIV). Jesus laid down His life and rose again so that we could spend eternity with Him in heaven and experience His absolute best on earth. If you would like to receive Jesus into your life, say the following prayer out loud and mean it from your heart.

Heavenly Father, I come to You admitting that I am a sinner. Right now, I choose to turn away from sin, and I ask You to cleanse me of all unrighteousness. I believe that Your Son, Jesus, died on the cross to take away my sins. I also believe that He rose again from the dead so that I might be forgiven of my sins and made righteous through faith in Him. I call upon the name of Jesus Christ to be the Savior and Lord of my life. Jesus, I choose to follow You and ask that You fill me with the power of the Holy Spirit. I declare that right now I am a child of God. I am free from sin and full of the right-eousness of God. I am saved in Jesus' name. Amen.

If you prayed this prayer to receive Jesus Christ as your Savior for the first time, please contact us on the Web at **www.harrisonhouse.com** to receive a free book.

Or you may write to us at
Harrison House • P.O. Box 35035 • Tulsa, Oklahoma 74153